Cornucopia

Leveraging Agriculture to Improve Health and Nutrition

D. Patrick Johnson

HAMILTON BOOKS

A member of
THE ROWMAN & LITTLEFIELD PUBLISHING GROUP
Lanham • Boulder • New York • Toronto • Plymouth, UK

Copyright © 2011 by
Hamilton Books
4501 Forbes Boulevard
Suite 200
Lanham, Maryland 20706
Hamilton Books Acquisitions Department (301) 459-3366

Estover Road
Plymouth PL6 7PY
United Kingdom

Contents

Illustrations

Preface

I became interested in the topics covered in *Cornucopia* about three years ago when I was first exposed to research by major food and health stalwarts such as Michael Pollan, Adam Drewnowski, Kelly Brownell, Greg Crister and many others. These authors and researchers were beginning to unravel a fascinating problem with far-reaching implications centered on how the American food system is making people sick. Since first picking up *The Omnivore's Dilemma* in early 2007, my curiosity in America's agricultural system steadily increased and I meticulously poured through the volume of literature that was being developed around this topic to learn about the connections between agriculture and health. I am very pleased to now be making my own contribution to this important national conversation with *Cornucopia*.

Thanks to support from the University of South Dakota, The Heritage Foundation and Booz Allen Hamilton, I dedicated a large portion of the past two years to understanding what had contributed to the current "perfect storm" environment where poor health is threatening our nation's future. In my research, I learned how tacit government programs support an amazingly complex and efficient food supply chain that is fueled by giant agribusinesses and industrial food manufacturers. This food system lies at the center of *Cornucopia*, a system that is delivering unhealthy calories to unknowing consumers every single day, leading to dietary diseases that cost the national economy hundreds of billions of dollars annually and also hold the honor of being the leading cause of preventable death in the country.

I am very grateful for everyone who has had a hand in asking the hard questions and promoting their belief that reforming America's agricultural system should be a top priority, because without it, effectively addressing health care, the environment, economic recovery or even national security will be impossible. The United States is at a crossroads right now, and reforming the American agricultural system is an integral step in creating a better future. The solutions outlined at the end of this book center on two key areas: 1) empowering citizens to make responsible food choices, and 2) developing a 21st Century Food System that optimizes local, regional and national production to enable and promote these decisions. Using the National School Lunch Program and Supplemental Nutrition Assistance Program to increase the availability of good, healthy food to those most in need is a great place to start.

My sincere hope in writing *Cornucopia* is to further communicate the pressing need for Americans to better understand the connection between health, nutrition and agriculture, sharing history's lessons in why we find ourselves at such a precipitous impasse and to offer prescriptive solutions to heal our bodies and the country.

Writing this book would not have been possible without my supportive and intelligent friends, family, colleagues and peers, and in specific I want to thank University of South Dakota Professors William Richardson, Randall Waldron, Jamison Rounds and Betty Smith for help, guidance, support and encouragement throughout researching and writing this book, Bill Beach and Rea Hederman at the Heritage Foundation for acting as a soundboard for ideas and for making a trip to South Dakota when I first presented the concepts covered in this book, Harvey Fliehs for teaching me how farming really works, my colleagues at Booz Allen Hamilton, Lynn Tjeerdsma and Dallas Tonsager at the USDA for providing me with a better understanding of farm programs and farm rural development support than I could have received from anyone else, Jane Grey for sharing her experiences at William & Mary and helping edit the entire manuscript, Dan English, Josh Tonsager and the rest of the Senatorial Offices of John Thune (R-SD), Tim Johnson (D-SD) and Sam Brownback (R-KS) for answering my questions and teaching me the difference between "politically possible" and the more common "politically impossible," Kate Fitzgerald at the National Sustainable Agricultural Coalition, and fellow South Dakotans Paul Erickson, Jake Mortenson, Sean Flynn and Andrew Christianson for blending their knowledge of politics, economics and agriculture every time I asked them to review parts of this book.

Thank-you also to my supportive family in Florida and South Dakota, my Russian surrogate family in D.C., and of course to Katya, for being with me day in and day out, helping me brainstorm and write this book, try out new recipes, and of course, clean up after me in the kitchen.

Chapter One

You Are What You Eat

It was not an accident that America was founded by farmers. While the percentage of Americans who farm has decreased from well over 90 percent back during America's founding to around one percent today, the relative importance of farms has remained steady and has quite probably increased. The incredible efficiency of the modern agriculture system is one of the biggest reasons why most Americans have never set foot on a farm, yet have more food than they know what to do with. America's farm sector has consistently been one of the fastest growing sectors of the American economy and is a hotbed of entrepreneurship and innovation. Going by the numbers, American agriculture adds at least $1 trillion annually to the national economy (13 percent of GDP) and employs over 17 percent of the workforce. Productivity gains in farming have also outpaced virtually all other sectors of the economy to the point where America's most competitive industries are now found scattered across the Midwest, as opposed to clustered on Wall Street or in Silicon Valley.

However, for all the fruits Americans have enjoyed from improvements in agriculture, the farm sector also masks some dark challenges that are now threatening to undermine the entire American way of life. Challenges with today's agricultural system are massive, yet just as most Americans have never thought about how farms provide for secure and prosperous futures across the country, today most Americans have no idea that farming is also leading to severe challenges the country is ill prepared for. These challenges extend beyond commonly held environmental, social and economic concerns to encapsulate something even more fundamental and more important—agriculture's impact on America's health. American agriculture is the biggest problem you have never heard of.

As crop yields have increased across the country—by an average of 50 percent each decade for many crops—reliance on natural resources and fossil fuels have reached all time highs. Agriculture now accounts for at least 20 percent of total fossil fuel use in the United States, and pesticides and fertilizers made from natural gas have become ubiquitous across the sector. Due to this reliance on fossil fuels in the agricultural industry, it takes approximately 10 calories worth of fossil fuel energy to produce one calorie of food today whereas half a century ago, farmers were able to produce that same calorie of food with just 1/20 of the fossil fuel inputs.

Food safety has also become a massive problem, as less than one percent of food is traceable from farm to fork. A complete lack of traceability in the complex supply chain that zips food across the country means that if a single bag of spinach is found to contain a food-borne disease, such as E-Coli, food manufactures must respond by recalling the entire crop off the market, as opposed to tracing a single bag of spinach back to the farm or processing plant where it was infected. Food recalls alone are estimated to cost the economy between $60 and $70 billion annually, along with the countless unnecessary deaths and illnesses that result from eating contaminated food.

Even with these massive food recalls, there are over 75 million cases of food-borne illnesses that occur each and every year leading to an estimated 325,000 hospital visits and around 5,000 deaths. These numbers, though, pale in comparison to the larger health imperative we face as a nation. Even with one of the best health care systems on the planet, the United States has become one of the world's most unhealthy countries. Fully two-thirds of the country is overweight or obese, and America now spends nearly as much money treating preventable dietary disease—some estimates place the total

A sample of consumer product recalls

2006			2007			2008		
E. Coli Spinach	Lettuce	Onions	E. Coli Mushrooms	Gr. Beef	Chicken	E. Coli Gr. Beef	Beef	
GMO Rice	Salmonella Chocolate	Choc. Nut	Salmonella Cantaloupe	Peanut Btr.	Snack Food	Salmonella Cantaloupe	Tomatoes	Jalapeños
			Botulism Canned Chilli	Baby Food	DEG Toothpaste	Listeria Pork	Melamine Formula	
			Melamine Pet Food	Dog Treats	Bird Flu Chicken	Lead Toys		

Figure 1.1.   IBM Analysis of Recent Food and Consumer Product Recalls.

for obesity, diabetes, hypertension and heart disease at over $500 billion annually—as the country spends on national defense. Most troubling of all: the country is not getting any healthier. Even with landmark healthcare legislation being signed into law by President Obama in early 2010, the causes of America's sickness are still being ignored. Of the over $2 trillion that is annually spent on healthcare in the U.S., more than 2/3 of the amount is spent treating chronic diseases.

As Harry Truman remarked in 1946, "no nation is healthier than their children or more prosperous than their farmers." While our farmers have indeed become quite prosperous, it is the health of America's children that is cause for greatest concern. Type II diabetes is forecasted to afflict one in three Americans born after 2000, and even today rising childhood obesity rates have caused First Lady Michelle Obama to make improving children's health her signature issue. Because of the proliferation of dietary diseases across the country, it is very possible that a child born today will have a life expectancy less than their parents, even after accounting for further advances in medical care.

The fundamental reason why America has become so unhealthy is because we have lost our connection between agriculture, health and nutrition. In no longer connecting with our food sources, we have severed the vital link of understanding how we impact the world around us and how that world in-turn impacts us. Intuitively, everyone knows that *you are what you eat*. Unsurprisingly, what America has chosen to eat has given the country the same symptoms as any other patient suffering from a serious dietary disease: an uncertain economic future, a life expectancy trending in reverse, and an environmental impact that is beginning to catch up to us. America is on an unsustainable track.

Most Americans can trace their roots back to farming, only needing to look over the past few generations to see a break in what was the common practice of living sustainably from the land. There is an urgent need to return to these roots as we begin to understand what has gone wrong in agriculture, and what we must do to fix the system.

Chapter Two

On the Farm

Groton is a town of less than 1,500 in northeast South Dakota's remote Brown County. Though the population has grown steadily over the past decade, most people live in Groton because their parents lived in Groton, and their grandparents before them. Though small, Groton High School annually fields some of the best sports teams in the state, gaining recognition for state and conference titles in basketball, football, volleyball, baseball and track—each of the big sports that serve to keep adolescents busy when they are not helping out on the farm. This is because in Groton, like much of the rural Midwest, farming dominates the economic landscape, and aside from the businesses that have sprouted up to cater to the local farm community, not much exists to keep kids occupied besides school, sports and a focus on continuing to rack up championship trophies.

Harvey Fliehs' family has been farming land in Groton for the past 60 years. His farm is one of the largest in Brown County, annually producing corn, wheat and soybeans on 10,000 acres. Harvey's father moved to Groton from Wisconsin following the end of World War II, a common strategy for farmers in the 1940s who abandoned Wisconsin's rocky soils for the prospect of more prosperous farms on the flat, treeless plains of the Dakotas.

With just $50 in his pocket and some government-backed GI loans, Harvey's father rented his first farm in 1951 on a plot of land that still serves as the family residence. Like most other farms of this era, Harvey Sr. ran a diversified farm, growing and raising spring wheat, barley, corn, oats, hogs and milk cows. Later that decade, he diversified further by replacing the milk cows with chickens and beef cattle.

Aside from the GI loans that helped Harvey Sr. get started on the farm, there was limited government intervention in the farming sector throughout the 1950s. This resulted in greater self-sufficiency in farm management, and led farmers to diversify their crop variety. Since many farming families depended on the yields of their land, it was important to ensure an ongoing income of produce to buffer the loss of one or two crops in a season. The idea of growing just one crop, and thus investing all of the farm's proverbial eggs in one basket, just didn't make sense. Most farms were diversified this way, as farmers sought to minimize the risk of investing all of their resources into one crop.

As the American economy continued to revert back to supporting a growing citizen base following the end of World War II, though, many government bureaucrats felt that even the modest degree of support being provided to farmers was too much. Ezra T. Benson, better known for later becoming President of The Church of Jesus Christ of Latter Day Saints, served as President Eisenhower's Secretary of Agriculture from 1953-1961, just as Harvey Sr. was starting to grow his farm. Benson strongly opposed the agricultural policies the Eisenhower administration had inherited and that offered modest support to Harvey Sr., believing that offering any government support to farmers amounted to "socialism." However, under Benson's stewardship, the price supports that were established under the 1949 Agricultural Act continued to provide farmers with a minimal layer of security. In 1954, Benson oversaw the introduction of flexible price supports for commodity programs that would further establish this precedent. These price supports could take the form of either subsidies or price controls, both of which have the consequence of keeping the market price for a given commodity steady at a set price, often above what the market would normally bear. Over time, these policies had a marked impact on the crops that would be grown on Harvey Sr.'s land.

Agriculture in the 1950s was marked by rapidly rising productivity, largely due to the adoption of mechanical farm equipment and advances in fertilizers and other chemical technologies. Between 1945 and 1960, the number of mules and horses used for farming decreased from 11.6 million to three million, while the number of mechanized tractors nearly doubled from 2.4 million to 4.7 million. These technological advances coincided with a period of consolidation in commercial agriculture, and though the share of the workforce employed in agriculture fell by over half, yields increased unrelentingly.

During Harvey's childhood, these technological gains eased the burden of labor on the farm, but did not detract from the essential, ongoing inputs from the entire family. Both the young and the elderly still pitched in, pulling their own weight by contributing individual skills and abilities to the continuing health of the farm. Though men and women worked in separate spheres and focused on specific jobs, each helped to support the farm significantly. During the harvest, crop collection became a family affair with full participation.

Through crop prices and productivity were low by today's standards, Harvey's father was able to expand his farming operation to around 3,000 acres of farmland, 500 acres of pasture, 1,500 feeder pigs and 200 cows as he continued to become more efficient at tilling the land. Wheat yields were around 20 bushels per acre (BPA) and corn yields were approximately 60-65 BPA.

After finishing his education and spending one year working for Hormel Foods in Idaho, Harvey returned to the farm in 1980 lured by a desire to run his own business. To Harvey, a career in agriculture presented lots of opportunities, and low cash rents meant that adding acreage was relatively easy. As Harvey expanded his farmland, consolidation in the pork industry led him to sell off his hogs and increase the number of beef cattle to 1,000 head. In the early part of the decade, the chicken industry also faced rapid consolidation, leading Harvey to abandon raising chickens as well. Corporations which began to absorb smaller farms, swallowing farmland and resources in a successful effort to gain a near monopoly on pork and poultry meat production, were easily able to out-compete these relatively marginal operations. Still, even without hogs and chickens, Harvey had his hands full focusing on growing grains and raising cattle. The mantra "get big or get out" was omnipresent throughout the entire agriculture sector, and farmers had begun applying management practices from the general economy by focusing on developing comparative advantages and only growing crops that presented the best economic returns.

Throughout the 1980s, spring wheat was grown as Harvey's largest cash crop, with approximately 40 percent of his land dedicated for corn. All of the corn that was grown was used in his cattle feedlot, and as Harvey's herd expanded, he bought additional corn from other farms to keep his cattle full. When Harvey's father had switched to beef cattle in the 1950s, cattle production in the United States was primarily grain and grass based. Beef cattle had naturally evolved on a grass-fed diet and developed metabolic and digestive tracts to process these foods. As meat consumption began increasing in the 1950s, American farmers began feeding their corn reserves to cattle in lieu of grass.

Cows and other grazing animals are naturally endowed with a rumen which serves as a sort of fermentation tank in the stomach. Naturally occurring bacteria in the rumen convert the cellulose from grasses into nutrients the cow can use. Unfortunately, the rumen did not evolve to digest corn, so as corn became a more significant part of the cattle's diet, powerful antibiotics were introduced to stifle the new bacterial growth in their digestive systems. Being fed a steady diet of nutritionally rich corn and a cocktail of antibiotics to aid in digestion, beef cattle could now reach slaughter weight in approximately half the time and also required less pasture land to graze.

Curiously, the relationships between inputs and outputs—what was used to produce crops and what was eventually harvested—began taking a backseat to productivity gains throughout this era as farms continued to "get big." To ask any farmer from Harvey Sr.'s era how the different parts of a farm fit together—how crop rotation helps to replenish nutrients in the soil, or how grazing chickens and cattle improve soil quality—would be to receive an answer founded on over 2,000 years of practice. But as farms began being run less like farms and more like industrial businesses, the focus naturally shifted away from *how* food was being produced, to *how much* was being produced.

Just as Harvey's farm began to grow, an economic crisis hit in 1981 that had severe and far-reaching impact. Throughout the 1970s, low interest rates and rising demand led many farmers to go deep into debt as they expanded their operations. American farm exports that had increased throughout the 1960s and 1970s plummeted between 1981 and 1983, falling by over 20 percent. Commodity prices also declined by over 20 percent during this same period, while interest rates increased to over 16 percent, in effect crippling the farm economy. Many farms were underwater.

By 1985, farmland in parts of the Midwest had fallen in value by over half, causing the USDA to intervene via commodity loans, various land set-aside programs and other subsidy payments designed to keep farmers solvent. Government intervention in the marketplace to control supply during this crisis was very important, and falling crop surpluses led to increasing commodity prices by the mid-1980s, helping farmers slowly recover from the crisis. During the second half of the 1980s, crop prices continued to swell and productivity on Harvey's farm increased uninhibited by low land rates. He was able to develop his property base further by acquiring neighboring farmland, renting and purchasing as much as possible. This allowed Harvey to introduce a new feedlot on the farm, a move which advantageously added value to the corn he grew. By the middle of the decade, his farm was yielding as much as 35 BPA of wheat and over 80 BPA of corn, a 50 percent improvement from the days when Harvey Sr. ran the farm.

The 1990s marked a change in production on Harvey's farm, as he switched to no-till farming practices and began to focus more exclusively on row crops. The introduction and widespread adoption of genetically modified organism (GMO) seeds by companies such as Monsanto and Advanced Genetic Sciences meant that hardy varieties of crops could now be grown in an array of conditions and climates. Harvey also invested in advanced pesticides and herbicides for weed control that helped him manage his land and crops each more effectively. With these fresh technological advances, Harvey's focus on improving his comparative fiscal advantage in growing row crops—corn and wheat—continued to keep him one step ahead.

For Harvey and thousands of other farmers, the 1990s would be remembered as a decade of increasingly advanced technology which ultimately resulted in reduced dependence on government subsidy. Tractors and combines, once functionally simple, were now equipped with yield monitors that could track production variability in fields. Once analyzed, this information could be used to further increase production by matching seeds with soil conditions to ensure optimal growing conditions. Harvey reacted to both these findings and market changes by cutting back on wheat production and increasing his investments in corn and soybeans. Harvey's corn and soybean yields jumped dramatically as he changed his crop strategy, increasing by over 50 percent from the previous decade.

The 1990s also saw relatively frequent fluctuations in commodity prices, but most years were good for Harvey and other farmers. The bets Harvey had placed on farmland throughout the 1980s began paying off, and he was now overseeing close to 8,000 acres of farmland, while also increasing the size of his feedlot to 4,000 head of cattle with an additional 400 stock cows. As farm incomes rose, reliance on subsidy programs became less important and farm program payments contributed to a smaller percentage of farm incomes. The USDA responded to these changes by introducing yield based subsidies, further supporting the increase in land values and rental rates.

The 2000s continued the technology march, and Harvey was able to introduce advanced GPS technologies on his farm to support variable rate technology that allowed for even greater control of fertilizer use and seed placement. Monitors are now used to control fertilizer, seed and chemical rates, with smaller amounts of these inputs still leading to increased crop yields. Harvey's no-till shift has also helped to preserve moisture in the soil, further supporting his move away from wheat and into more row crops such as corn. With more precision planting, yields on Harvey's farm increased while the amount of seeds and fertilizers used decreased. Harvey invested heavily in technology for his farm, even as the price of new combines and tractors continued to increase.

Harvey now farms 10,000 acres divided pretty evenly between corn and soybeans, with about 10 percent devoted for wheat. Responding to environmental concerns, the EPA adopted new legislation that mandated stricter waste control from cattle feed lots. The cost for Harvey to comply with the new law would have been over $500,000, an investment Harvey chose not to make, opting instead to get rid of his 4,000 cows. To address these and other requirements, a remarkable pattern of consolidation in cattle feedlots emerged to the point where now, most cattle feedlots in South Dakota and in other parts of the country hold a minimum of 10,000 cattle.

Related to this consolidation in the cattle industry, ethanol plants began to spread across the Midwest as cattle ranchers and stock yards purchased ethanol by-products to feed their ever-expanding cattle operations. As a result, many farmers—including Harvey—began to market 100 percent of corn production to local ethanol plants instead. Now, the 4,500 areas of corn Harvey's farm produces annually are sold in their entirety to a local ethanol plant.

In the 30 years that Harvey has been farming, yields on most crops have increased by 250 percent. Across his fields, corn yields are approaching 200 BPA. Amazingly, most farming operations during this time managed to increase in size as they became evermore specialized and idiosyncratic. The efficiencies of technology have been offset by increased food demand, so margins have remained relatively constant at about $50 per acre. Even so, Harvey expects yields to double over the next decade as technology continues to supplement improved growing techniques and even-greater specialization.

After graduating with honors from Iowa State University in 2005 and brief stints working in New York City and Los Angeles, Harvey's son Trey returned back to Groton this past year to help run the family farm, preparing for the day when Harvey retires and turns the farm over to him fulltime. By then, Trey might be splitting time between sitting in the rafters at Groton High School watching his children rack up athletic championships, while quietly growing and improving on his father's and grandfather's legacy of running a successful farming operation in a quite patch of South Dakota prairie.

Chapter Three

America's Cornucopia

Harvey's South Dakota farm has gone from producing approximately 160,000 bushels of corn annually in the mid-1980s to over 800,000 bushels today. The democratization of technology in farming, though, has also meant that Harvey has not unilaterally benefited from the increased efficiencies he has introduced on his farm. In Illinois, Iowa, Wisconsin and every other farming state, yields have increased by similar margins with farms producing more and more corn every year. All told, the millions of acres of farmland planted with corn each year produce over 13 billion bushels of corn. At current yields, each one of these bushels contains nearly 50lbs of food (one acre of corn equates to nearly 10,000lbs!), however it is important to note that this corn is not the typical sweet corn you would find at the grocery store. Most of these 13 billion bushels are commercial grade corn that has been engineered for high yields and for versatility in manufacturing. Basically, the corn being grown is less a food and more of an industrial input. So, with all of the advances in agriculture, growing corn has become the easy part. Figuring out what to do with such a massive supply of the crop has been a different story.

Based on America's abundance of corn, it should be no surprise that over the past three decades corn-derived products have begun appearing in more and more foods as prices have continued to fall resulting from the continually increasing supply. With corn prices remaining low, food producers have become increasingly dependent on it in all phases of the food chain as a "cheap input." As Bunny Crumpacker points out in her Washington Post review of Michael Pollan's 2006 bestselling book *The Omnivore's Dilemma*:

> American cattle fatten on corn. Corn also feeds poultry, pigs and sheep, even farmed fish . . . In addition to dairy products from corn-fed cows and eggs from corn-fed chickens, cornstarch, corn oil and corn syrup make up key ingredients

in prepared food. High-fructose corn syrup sweetens everything from juice to toothpaste. Even the alcohol in beer is corn-based. Corn is in everything from frozen yogurt to ketchup, from mayonnaise and mustard to hot dogs and bologna, from salad dressings to vitamin pills.

This phenomenon has led Pollan to state that if the adage "you are what you eat" is true, then Americans would be corn. Pollan's research led to the astounding realization that over one-quarter of all the items found in a typical grocery store are either derived from corn or contain corn-based products.

In order to attract income from this cheap and abundant resource of corn, a variety of micro industries have popped up around the nation. Ethanol plants are one of the most egregious examples, with ethanol production increasing from 175 million to 9 billion barrels in just 30 years. Over 170 ethanol plants are currently in operation nationwide, a significant increase from the 50 in existence just 10 years ago.

The American relationship with ethanol production can actually be traced to the start of the 20th century, and though it had promising beginnings, gasoline use proved to be a more preferable economic choice. Henry Ford's first automobile, the Quadricycle, was actually designed to run purely on ethanol, making Ford a major advocate of lifting prohibition during that period (the distillation process to make grain-based alcohol mirrors that for the production of ethanol). By the Model T's release a decade later, automotives were designed to take any combination of gasoline and/or ethanol, but with the availability of cheap gasoline, motorists and manufactures eventually shifted their attention away from ethanol.

In concept, using ethanol to power American vehicles has always been an attractive idea. Its production has been supported by environmental activists and politicians alike as it is a "cleaner" fuel than petroleum gasoline and an additional source of income for farmers producing corn. National security hawks like to point out that producing fuel domestically limits America's exposure to oil imports, and thus enhances national security. Unfortunately, not all of the facts around ethanol production support these claims, and were it not for heavy government intervention and support, ethanol would cease to be a viable fuel source in the United States.

To begin, the cost of producing a gallon of ethanol would be cost-prohibitive if not for government subsidies that amount to $0.45 per gallon. Further government subsidies, loan guarantees, tax incentives and other policies have also been enacted over the last decade to insulate domestic ethanol producers from foreign competition and encourage increased production. For example, a $0.54 tariff on ethanol imports helps negate the fact that other countries, most notably Brazil, are much more competitive in their ethanol production. While these measures have made the fuel seem cost-competitive with gasoline in the U.S., its actual price is significantly greater and is not currently sustainable.

Ethanol presents other concerns that the government has not been able to offset. Since the 1970s, ethanol's use has increased steadily and currently most gasoline sold in the United States is blended with 10 percent ethanol. Two major milestones that have further cemented this use of ethanol include amendments to the Clean Air Act in 1992 and the Energy Policy Act of 2005. The former sought to decrease carbon monoxide emissions by mandating the use of methyl tertiary butyl ether, infamously known as MTBE. Amid environmental concerns, it was found that MTBE was contaminating groundwater sources, a discovery which led U.S. gasoline refiners and suppliers to begin utilizing ethanol as a way to meet new government emission mandates. Now, MTBE is currently banned in approximately 20 states, and cost estimates to clean up contaminated water sources range from $1-15 billion.

Unfortunately, the way emissions are calculated for ethanol paint an incomplete picture about the actual environmental cost. When the Bush White House began advocating for the increased use of corn-based ethanol in gasoline, the price of corn hovered around $2.00 per bushel. Farmers, sensing the inevitable demand shift that would result from this new government support, responded by cultivating more corn. This steep increase in supply was matched by growth in the ethanol industry, such that by 2008, the amount of ethanol being produced in the United States had more than tripled over the previous five year period. Even so, we remain reliant on the same fossil fuels which we were meaning to transition away from. The ethanol which was supposed to help lead this transition has not stopped oil use from continuing on the same trajectory, and in fact has increased our reliance on foreign oil in many areas. This results from the fact that the corn used to produce this ethanol is still hinged on massive inputs of oil and natural gas. Currently, around 40 percent of total U.S. corn production is converted into ethanol, yet even if the entire U.S. corn crop was dedicated solely for ethanol, the increased output would equate to under 10 percent of total U.S. oil imports.

As the price of corn rose with increased market demand, farmers recognized the rising cost as an opportunity for additional revenue. Initially at $2 per bushel, corn was only grown on lands where yield outweighed the cost of production. But as this price suddenly increased by a factor of two, land which was formerly set aside for growing other crops or carbon sequestration was now tilled for its weight in corn. In addition to this transition of natural habitat to arable farmland, the actual production of ethanol from corn requires large amounts of fossil fuel inputs. To continue growing amid these real and serious concerns, the ethanol business has required direct government support, slick marketing campaigns and a healthy dose of fuzzy math.

David Pimenthal is a leading agricultural expert from Cornell University and an outspoken critic of ethanol. Dr. Pimenthal has referred to ethanol production as "sustainable subsidized food burning" since the amount of farmland needed to produce fuel for a single automobile annually could theoretically be used to feed seven people for an entire year. Dr. Pimenthal's research has revealed, quite alarmingly, that it requires more energy to produce one gallon of ethanol than is actually contained in the ethanol itself! To be exact, 131,000 BTUs are needed to make one gallon of ethanol, yet this gallon of ethanol contains only 77,000 BTUs worth of energy. All these facts illuminate a crucially important question: does producing fuel which loses over 70 percent of its initially energy value make any economic, environmental or strategic sense?

A helpful comparison to understanding the economics at play here can be defined by this hypothetical scenario: Imagine the United States government was concerned about cutting down trees that were being converted into paper dollar bills. In response, the government then decides to offer incentives for citizens to trade in paper money for metal coins. However, in order to smelt the metal coins, an even greater number of trees have to be cut down to fire power plants. This nonsensical loop which uses large amounts of energy to produce a fraction of the input is, unfortunately, a reality which needs to be addressed with ethanol production. Though the Federal Government has decided this is a fair economic trade in the case of ethanol, without sustained support the entire industry would go bankrupt.

The food for fuel concerns centered on ethanol use also deserve increased scrutiny, and a 2008 World Bank Report found that "the most important factor" in rising global food prices "was the large increase in biofuel production in the U.S. and the E.U." The report did little to alleviate concerns of a global food crisis spurned by the burgeoning ethanol industry, while also introducing new ethical considerations into the corn-based ethanol debate to complement the political, economic and environmental concerns already addressed.

All these statistics paint a pretty damning picture against ethanol use, but is the evidence really this clear? Well, that depends on the data sets being used in the calculation and what assumptions the researchers are making. For instance, on Harvey's farm, his 800,000+ bushels of corn are transformed into three million gallons of ethanol. Amazingly, Harvey's net fuel use to grow and transport that corn is just 30,000 gallons, leading to a net fuel gain of approximately 2.97 million gallons. Viewed at in this light, the case against ethanol starts to get a little murky. The truth is that both ethanol advocates and their opposition design their studies and calculations (with corresponding assumptions) to communicate desirable outcomes. As with most other challenges in farm policy, in assessing the value of ethanol, everything is more complicated than it seems.

Corn is popular around the world and is grown on every continent other than Antarctica. Still, America's addiction to corn is unprecedented on both global and historical scales. The rapidly growing ethanol industry is one example of how shrewd businessmen and savvy politicians have capitalized on abundant corn, trading votes for business. While some Native American tribes across America's prairies used corn as a currency hundreds of years ago, the use of corn as a political currency today is symbolic of the powerful grip the commodity has held over the United States since before its founding.

Chapter Four

How We Got Fat, Part I

In addition to the ethanol plants that have been gulping up excess corn, an entirely new food supply chain has also evolved based on the premise of this cheap and available resource. As the United States begins to grapple with the consequences of an increasingly sedentary and unhealthy populous, much more attention is being directed to help determine what has contributed in making the country sick. Ironically, the politicians asking these questions need not look far in finding the answer.

Bad government policies have compounded to create a perfect storm environment where unhealthy foods are cheap and readily available, preventative medical care is non-existent or cost-prohibitive and the companies that are doing the most harm somehow exert the most political influence in Washington. The United States was founded on the basic premise that people should be free to choose in all aspects of their lives. This tenet has helped create an incredibly vibrant society where entrepreneurship, innovation and diverse minds have all coalesced to create a truly special and unique country. The absence of government intervention in many sectors of the economy and civil society have permitted people and businesses to flourish, allowing consumers to effectively vote with their wallets to determine the direction of the country. In many cases, this arrangement has worked remarkably well. Unfortunately, this is not the case in agriculture.

America's agricultural system has progressed steadily over the past century. In 1900, 38 percent of the workforce labored on farms to keep the country fed. The same agricultural advancements that have made Harvey's operations so much more efficient have streamlined agricultural production to the point where today, just one percent of the American population farms professionally. Amazingly, this small subset of the population produces such a tremendous amount of food that it requires a good deal of innovation to figure out how to use all of it.

As agriculture has always played a prominent role in the nation's economy (the majority of our forefathers did, after all, come from farming backgrounds), the government has historically been somewhat more involved in its promotion and sustainment than other sectors of the economy. The sorts of government intervention that have encouraged agriculture include loan guarantees, crop subsidies, special tax incentives and other payment guarantees. For the most part, these programs were designed to maintain a viable and competitive agricultural sector and the majority of farmers required a certain level of government support to just break even. For most of our nation's history, farming was not a way to get rich, and while farmers might have owned large plots of land, their income and welfare was largely tied up in maintaining the operations of the farm.

The United States Department of Agriculture (USDA) was founded in 1862 in the midst of the Civil War by President Abraham Lincoln. While Lincoln referred to the USDA as "the people's department," he choose to not confer cabinet status to its secretary. Though Lincoln himself was from a rural background, he maintained strong beliefs that while farmers were an integral part of the nation, the government's primary responsibility to them was to maintain a system that allowed farms to flourish. In fact, speaking to the Wisconsin State Agricultural Society in September 1859, Lincoln remarked:

> I presume I am not expected to employ the time assigned to me in the mere flattery of the farmers, as a class. My opinion of them is that, in proportion to numbers, they are neither better nor worse than any other people. In the nature of things they are more numerous than any other class; and I believe there really are more attempts at flattering them than any other; the reason of which I cannot perceive, unless it be that they can cast more votes than any other . . .

While the fact that farmers "cast more votes than any other (class)" may not have influenced Lincoln much, the political clout of farmers and farm lobbies have played a decisive role both before and after Honest Abe's administration, with just a few notable exceptions.

The way the USDA has evolved over the past 150 years is representative of the changing role of government involvement in the agricultural sector. The USDA was initially founded "to acquire and diffuse among the people of the United States useful information on subjects concerned with agriculture in the most general and comprehensive sense of that word." At the outset, the USDA primarily engaged in research and helped with the dissemination of best practice tips and techniques to farmers. By the twentieth century, the USDA had expanded to also include conservation and road building among its primary duties. The USDA has since grown with the rest of the Federal Government and is now one of the largest Federal agencies, employing over 100,000 people and maintaining an annual budget of nearly $100 billion.

The Constitution neither holds special exemptions for farmers nor calls for government intervention in the agricultural sector. This is one of the reasons why, when commodity prices plummeted in the 1920s following the end of the First World War, President Calvin Coolidge vetoed the McNary-Haugen Farm Relief Bill that would have introduced price-fixing and other government guarantees to farmers. In his veto message, Coolidge said:

> I do not believe that upon serious consideration the farmers of America would tolerate the precedent of a body of men chosen solely by one industry who, acting in the name of the Government, shall arrange for contracts which determine prices, secure the buying and selling of commodities, the levying of taxes on that industry, and pay losses on foreign dumping of any surplus . . . There is no reason why other industries—copper, coal, lumber, textiles, and others—in every occasional difficulty should not receive the same treatment by the Government. Such action would establish bureaucracy on such a scale as to dominate not only the economic life but the moral, social, and political future of our people.

Ultimately, the Great Depression drastically changed both the landscape of the American economy and the level of governmental intervention society would tolerate. The Depression effectively destroyed the responsible historical precedents which had been established by the Constitution and Presidents Lincoln and Coolidge regarding farm policy.

Responding to widespread unemployment, hunger and general malaise, President Herbert Hoover fulfilled a campaign promise to "establish for our farmers an income equal to those of other occupations" by creating the Federal Farm Board in 1929 and investing it "with responsibilities and resources such as never before been conferred by our government in assistance to any industry." The Farm Board established price guarantees for many crops and commodities through targeted market interference by limiting production and buying and storing surplus crops. For example, the Act established floor prices on wheat and cotton, which led many farmers who had been growing other crops to switch to wheat or cotton because of the stable price guarantee. The overproduction of these crops further contributed to lower prices, making even more farmers directly dependent on government intervention to sell their crops at a profit.

Responding to popular discontent over these policies, Congressman James Beck remarked in 1932, "The Farm Board is clearly the most costly and inexcusable legislative folly in our history." The newly-formed farm lobby also put its weight behind higher tariff and import controls to further isolate themselves from international competition by supporting the Smoot-Hawley Act of 1930. As reported by the State Department, this Act provoked retaliatory measures from European nations that helped result in a 66 percent drop in trade between the U.S. and Europe from 1929 and 1934.

President Franklin Roosevelt further entrenched government intervention in the agricultural sector through his Agricultural Adjustment Act in 1933. This Act attempted to correct the crop imbalance by restricting production of certain crops, sometimes by paying farmers not to cultivate all their land. The primary effects of this policy were to decrease supply while demand remained constant leading to an increase in price. The Act also established the Agricultural Adjustment Administration to oversee subsidy payouts. In United States v. Butler in 1936, the Supreme Court ruled the Agricultural Adjustment Act unconstitutional because it paid farmers for decreasing their production by taxing companies that bought farm products. However, a slightly modified version of the bill ended up being passed in 1938 that worked around the Supreme Court's ruling.

During Richard Nixon's administration in the early 1970s, the aim of subsidies shifted from discouraging overproduction to a system that blatantly encouraged crop surpluses as a way to combat the high food prices that had crept back in the early 1970s. Food prices rose as the result of Nixon's 1972 grain belt deal with the Soviet Union which sent millions of pounds of American grain to the U.S.S.R., in addition to corresponding droughts in the farm belt that drastically limited the domestic supply of commodities.

Ever the shrewd politician, Nixon ordered Earl "Rusty" Butz, then Secretary of Agriculture, to take whatever actions necessary to drive down the price of food and limit his administration's political exposure to the impending food crisis. Butz responded by introducing direct payments for certain commodity crops that incentivized farmers to dump their harvests directly in the market rather than hold back surpluses to keep prices higher. Butz also believed that farming needed to mirror the rest of the economy through increased consolidation and larger farming operations. Butz's "get big or get out" mandate had profound impacts in helping Harvey's family grow their farm, but as the size of farms increased so too did their influence on government.

Current farm policy is based largely on the precedents established by Presidents Hoover, Roosevelt and Nixon and still employs many of the same mechanisms to control price and production levels. Over 90 percent of subsidies support just five crops: wheat, cotton, corn, soybeans and sugar. Just as the price guarantees established by the Farm Board in 1929 led to the overproduction of wheat and cotton, current policies have led to a surplus of those five crops at the expense of other foodstuffs.

Today, crop prices are high enough so that Harvey, like most other farm-ers, does not have much need or reliance on direct government support. In contrast, Harvey Sr.'s decision to stop raising livestock and instead focus on a few major cash crops was at least indirectly influenced by government farm policy post-Nixon. Farming is still a relatively low-margin business, but once the land and major equipment is purchased, the cost of farming a given acre is pretty low. The large fixed costs which are associated with running a successful commercial farm, though, have led to the further consolidation of most farming industries and prevented small- and mid- sized farms from truly taking hold.

While current government farm programs might have little direct influ-ence on the types of crops Harvey and other farmers choose to grow, this consolidation in the agriculture industry has changed the business for the worse. While the country is only now starting to recognize the unforeseen legacies imposed by past government farm policies, "get big or get out" has meant that today, just five companies control almost 50 percent of the $1 trillion agriculture business. These five companies and their armies of lobbyists in Washington invest hundreds of millions of dollars each year into promoting policies that help their business. Unsurprisingly, they keep getting what they want.

Thinking of agriculture as a set of concentric circles can be helpful in imagining who really has power over the direction the industry takes. In the first circle, agriculture is a market fueled by personal production, such as when Harvey would bring in eggs from the henhouse each morning for break-fast. In this circle, production and consumption are tied so that the same per-son growing the food ends up consuming it. As you move out to the second circle of agriculture, there is a direct relationship between the producer and consumer, such as at a farmers market where products are directly exchanged.

Continuing out, the third circle introduces an additional degree of separa-tion between production and consumption, such as the section in the local grocery store that sells products directly sourced from local farms. The forth tier is where large volume aggregation and distribution occurs. In this circle, big firms such as Sysco Foods purchase bulk products from farmers and then sell those products to supermarkets, where only then are they available to American households. And finally, in the fifth circle are the major players, those five corporations that control nearly half of the entire agricultural mar-ket through global production, aggregation and distribution. These firms took "get big or get out" to a new level as they source and purchase inputs from across the globe, consolidate them in giant warehouses across the country, steer these commodities to processing facilities and then ship their manufac-tured products to supermarkets across the country.

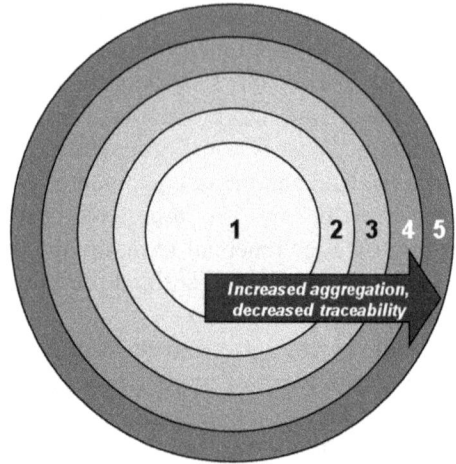

Figure 4.1. Tiers of Agricultural Production.

As you move out across the circles, the level of traceability decreases. One of the key reasons why only one percent of food is traceable from farm to fork today is because such a large percentage of food ultimately comes from the giant corporations in the fifth tier.

Another trend illustrated by these circles is the farmer's economic share of food production. In the first tier, the farmer directly benefits from his/her labor by consuming the food produced. In the second tier, the farmer enjoys 100 percent of the money earned by selling food directly to consumers. Even at the third tier, farmers are able to enjoy higher margins on their products sold at supermarkets as there is only one link separating them from that sale in the supply chain. But in the fifth tier where the business is ultimately driven, farmers end up earning around a mere 10 percent of the total purchase price of the food they grew, with the rest of the money going to various "value added" activities such as refinement, processing, shipping and marketing.

If farmers stand to earn so much more money by selling food directly to consumers, then why do we not see more farmers markets and cooperatives? After all, in a low margin business such as farming, each percentage makes a big difference to the bottom line. Among the barriers that face small and mid-sized farms as they seek to sell directly to consumers are liability laws in many large organizations (schools, businesses, government agencies) that require food purchasing to be completed by firms that maintain overly burdensome levels of liability insurance (what small farmer is going have a $4 million liability policy?). For many small and mid-sized farms, time is as great a constraint as money or an insurance policy. While some communities have well-established farmers markets and cooperatives that facilitate the sale of food directly to consumers, this infrastructure does not exist in many parts of the country. After considering the time and effort expended in selling directly to consumers, many farmers find that selling to large-scale distributors is a more worthwhile investment.

Back in the tiers of agriculture illustration, each concentric circle can also define different types of food being produced and consumed. In actuality, the five sections can be broken into two groups: the first, consisting of tiers one, two and three, is characterized largely by fresh, whole foods. Here, food is typically sold fresh out of the ground with little or no processing. The outermost two tiers, four and five, consist primarily of foods that have been processed and manufactured. Of course, there are exceptions to this rule. Sysco Foods, and their competitors, are not only in the business of selling boxed, frozen foods, but also make a significant portion of their revenue by selling fresh fruits and vegetables. This produce, though seemingly fresh, is deceptively packaged and preserved to extend shelf-life abnormally beyond the produce that can be purchased at a farmers market or grown at home. Still, this fares better in comparison with the final tier, in which the types of food being produced and sold are almost entirely manufactured and carry questionable nutritional value. It seems that "value add" comes with nutritional deficit.

Due to the scope and scale of the few giant firms in the fifth and outermost tier, manufactured and processed foods form the shaky foundation for much of the diet across the United States today—the American diet.

Chapter Five

The American Diet

The American diet makes people fat. Over the past few decades, waistlines across the country have expanded at ever-faster rates, and diet-related diseases now cost the United States hundreds of billions of dollars annually. Under the guise of political correctness, millions of overweight Americans have continued getting fatter, while any plea from doctors, journalists or politicians has fallen on deaf ears. Of course, the underlying cause of why Americans are getting fatter is pretty simple to understand: over the past 30 years, food consumption has risen by 16 percent and the average American now consumes 523 more calories per day than in 1970. But there is more to the story than just calories.

When it comes to health, where calories come from is just as important as the number consumed. Doctors and dieticians are among the first to tell you that America's fixation with calories is itself a dangerous eating disorder. A large percentage of Americans assess their diet based on number of calories or nutrients alone, a recent phenomenon so widespread that scholars and scientists have even devised a new term to describe it: *nutritionism*.

At its base level, nutritionism occurs when the nutrients that comprise any given piece of food are deconstructed out of the "whole food" context. Nutritionism is why food labels are so difficult to comprehend and why so many ingredients and percentages are listed for even simple foods. Thought you were just eating an apple? Not exactly. Nutritionism deconstructs the nutrients that comprise the calories in that apple to their most simple form. Now, based on a 2,000 calorie diet, the 80 calories in your typical Red Delicious apple actually constitutes seven percent of the daily recommended number of carbohydrates, largely delivered through 17 grams of sugar. But as common sense should tell us, there's more to that apple than just these numbers.

A recent survey revealed that the majority of American consumers, and 60 percent of women, always or usually read food labels. When looking at these food labels, studies have shown that 59 percent of consumers are concerned about a product's fat content, 52 percent by the number of calories, 37 percent by sugar and 31 by the amount of salt. With numbers such as these, it is no wonder that American food corporations devote so many resources towards manufacturing foods that have labels such as *"Low Fat!," "Less Sodium!," "½ the Sugar!"* and so on.

Nutritionism is dangerous exactly because it deconstructs food, erasing nutrients from the picture while overly emphasizing caloric intake. According to nutritionism, eaters could just consume empty calories all day, supplement that diet with a few vitamins before bed, and be perfectly healthy. In fact, food manufacturers have sought to simplify this relationship even further by injecting soft drinks and other processed foods with vitamins and minerals. This was the original concept behind the creation of Wonder Bread, when food manufacturers at Continental Bakery were able to take nutritionally-worthless white flour, and then "enrich" it with some of the nutrients it lacked. Wonder Bread flew off the shelf as parent's thought they had found a winning combination of food that tasted good to kids, and was also healthy.

While good in theory, nutritionism has not worked because not all 2,000 calorie diets are equal. Research has shown that calories consumed from real foods are significantly healthier than a diet of manufactured foods, even if the nutrition labels add up to the same thing. The concept at play here is called "food synergy" and it has been used to show (by researchers such as David Jacobs, Lynn Steffen, and others) that certain combinations of nutrients in foods are healthier when consumed together rather than individually. Nutritionism has yet to realize that when assessing the nutritional value of certain foods, the sum truly is greater than the individual parts.

In most parts of the world, the word "diet" even has a different meaning than what it refers to in the United States. In Greece, Italy or Spain, "diet" conjures up images of Mediterranean foods—olive trees, wine, cheeses, pastas, ripe vegetables. In Asia, each country also has a specific diet, from the pho soups that are the staple in Vietnam to rice-based dishes throughout China. Think of Mexico, and corn-based tortillas, rich salsas and beans with rice all come to mind. Each of these national diets have a few common characteristics: 1) they are all regionally suited to rely on local crops, 2) the attention paid to calories is virtually non-existent, and 3) the people who live off them are uniformly healthier than Americans.

The U.S. has never had a "national diet." Much of this is tied to the fact America doesn't have an official national language either—America's citizenry immigrated from all over the world, each bringing a unique culture and heritage that is somewhere represented in America's great mixing pot. Unfortunately, the diet that emerged from this rich history has neither form nor consistency, and is often viewed internationally as a combination of McDonald's, Pizza Hut and KFC. Also unique to the American diet is where the actual eating takes place. Amazingly, nearly 20 percent of all eating for 18-50 year olds, across demographics, is completed in the car.

With all of the availability of fast food and processed foods, the American diet is certainly a convenient and cheap one. Americans spend under 10 percent of their net income on food, compared with close to 15 percent for both the French and Italians and over 17 percent for the Spanish. Additionally, the amount of time spent preparing and cleaning-up after making food has fallen from over one hour per day in the 1960s to under 30 minutes today. While the American diet appears cheap, it is interesting to note the variance in food spending versus health care spending that has occurred over the past 50 years. In 1960, Americans spent around 17.5 percent of income on food and about 5 percent on health care. Now, these percentages have switched places with 16 percent of national income spend on health care while only 9.9 percent is dedicated for food.

Tellingly, it has been shown that when people immigrate to the United States from other countries they gain weight, while Americans who move abroad lose weight. America's dietary traditions are the underlying reason why 64 percent of adults over the age of 20 are currently classified as overweight or obese. While many factors have contributed to this staggering number, the basic premise is easy to explain: Americans now consume more food energy (calories) than they expend. But the economics of eating are a two-way street. Before that McDonalds hamburger is sold to a hungry patron, the ingredients had to be grown, processed, manufactured and shipped.

As with most other countries, it is important to consider the environment when questioning why Americans eat the way they do. What is grown in America's farm fields or raised in its pastures is the first link in today's increasingly-complicated and interconnected food chain. Guidelines, such as the ubiquitous food pyramid, help inform Americans about what they should eat on a daily basis, but exert little, if any, influence over the types of foods that are produced to begin with. The fundamental link between what is grown and then later consumed attracts surprisingly little attention in today's diet-centric environment. Based on both consolidation and specialization in the farming industry and government support of a few key staple crops, it should be no surprise that Americans get 80 percent of their daily calories from just four crops, with wheat and corn alone accounting for approximately 60 percent.

Chapter Six

How We Got Fat, Part II

As mentioned previously, in 2009, the United States produced over 13 billion bushels of corn. Of this corn, approximately 20 percent was exported, with the remaining 11 billion bushels used for feedstock (5.5 billion bushels), ethanol production (4.2 billion) and other commercial food uses (1.3 billion). To put this last number into perspective, 1.3 billion bushels of corn equates to over 2,000 ears of corn per year for every man, woman and child in America.

Obviously it is not possible to eat this much corn, so in order to process the reserves, food manufacturers have been increasingly innovative in finding ways to integrate corn into all stages of their food supply chains. Approximately 17,000 new food products are created annually, and around 8,000 of these contain corn or a corn-based derivative. Corn is now the primary ingredient used in commercial feed lots for cattle, poultry, sheep, pigs—even for farmed fish! As a sweetener in form of high-fructose corn syrup (HFCS), corn appears in ice cream, ketchup, toothpaste, soft drinks, bread, jelly preserves, potato chips, breakfast cereal, canned soup, salad dressing and yes, even McDonald's hamburger buns. The list goes on, *ad nauseum*.

When considering the application of the "you are what you eat" principle, American's truly are becoming walking stalks of corn, like Michael Pollan suggested. Just consider: applying this logic to the typical McDonald's cheeseburger, the bun, ketchup and mustard all contain HFCS, while the meat patty and cheese both originated from corn-fed cattle. *And you thought you were eating a cheeseburger?*

As thousands of American farmers and the all-powerful National Corn Growers Association will attest, in-and-of-itself, corn is not a bad thing. Advancements in how corn is grown and processed account for some of the biggest reasons for why crop yields have increased to the disproportionate levels they have reached today, which support the reliance of millions on

Billion bushels

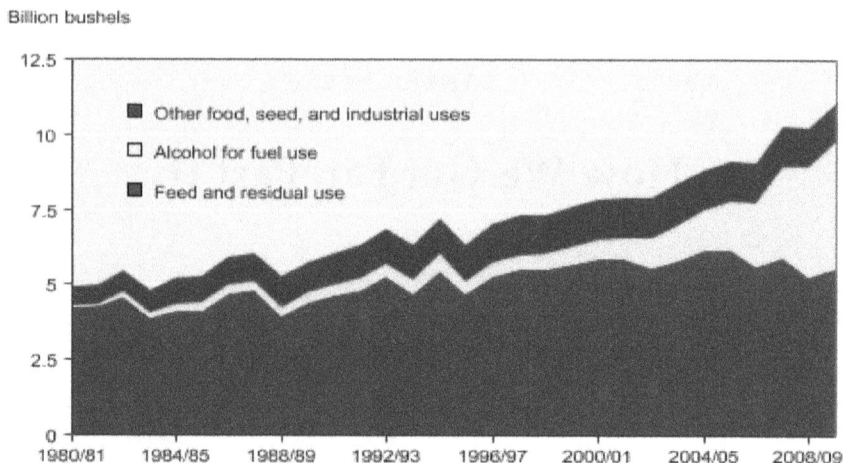

Figure 6.1.   Domestic U.S. Corn Use Breakdown.

American-grown corn to fortify local diets. The crop accounts for a large percentage of foreign food aid to Africa and Asia, even as the abundance of corn locally creates micro-industries which focus specifically on processing it for use in other products. Even with these caveats, Americans are now victim to an overabundance of corn, and many health professionals are seeing the consequence of its prevalence in the American diet. This is especially true in the case of corn-based sweeteners, which are partially responsible for why the United States is becoming the Land of the Fat.

A cornucopia of corn. The story of how and why corn came to play such a prominent role in America's, and by extension, the World's, food supply has been privy to numerous books, academic studies and even Congressional debates over the past few years. As was discussed earlier, prior government support of corn certainly helped promote and establish corn as a staple crop. Had the government decided to discourage its use as feed for livestock (again, corn stock is unnatural for cattle and requires supplementary antibiotics to keep cows from getting sick, even as it helps them fatten up more quickly), then it is certain that vastly less corn would currently be produced.

Without discounting legitimate reasons for why farmers have opted to grow ever-greater quantities of corn, prior U.S. Government support in the form of farm subsidies and price supports helped created numerous incentives for growing corn. And grow corn they did! As American farmers produced ever-greater quantities of corn, increasing market demands, such as the government-backed ethanol boom, helped offset much of the production increases.

Resulting from this arrangement, an industrial food system has developed that takes these five subsidized staples (wheat, cotton, corn, soybeans and sugar) and then manufactures them into scores of food products that line the shelves in grocery stores across the country. Looking on the back of any food label, anyone without a Ph.D. in chemistry would have a difficult time comprehending what was in their food. For example, the ingredients in Kellogg's Corn Flakes read: Milled Corn, Sugar, Malt Flavoring, High Fructose Corn Syrup, Salt, Iron, Niacinamide, Sodium Ascorbate and Ascorbic Acid (Vitamin C), Pyridoxinehydrochloride (Vitamin B6), Riboflavin (Vitamin B2), Thiaminhydrochloride (Vitamin B1), Vitamin A Palmitate, Folic Acid, Vitamin B12 and Vitamin D. *What?*

The process of manufacturing Corn Flakes is much like that of any other industrial good: with a number of inputs (many of which in this instance were derived from corn), a product is created that attracts consumers through good taste and an inexpensive price tag, both of which make it easy for the product to be marketed and sold. As an ancillary benefit, manufactured food can also be easily shipped anywhere around the world, able to survive a much longer shelf life than fresh fruits or vegetables.

When a prospective consumer looks on the back of Corn Flakes and decides to make the purchase, they are doing so with an incomplete understanding of how the Corn Flakes will be processed and used by their body. No matter what the name says, Corn Flakes are not simply flakes of corn and are not processed by the body the same way as an ear of corn. This misconception is fueled by the concept of nutritionism, which paints an incomplete picture of the true value whole foods carry over manufactured alternates. Indeed, many nutrition advocates believe that nutrition labels end up doing more harm than good, as consumers are only drawn to eye-catching jargons such as *0% Fat!, Organic! Sugar Free! Vitamin Enriched! 100% Natural!* or *New and Improved!*

While the business case for producing Corn Flakes is clear, the question of why the country is hooked on processed foods is a little more complicated. Over the years, various government policies have at least tacitly encouraged the production of certain crops at the expense of others. Farming is somewhat zero-sum, meaning that if land is used for growing corn, then that same land cannot be used for growing something else. When a government mandate is enacted, such as a call to produce more corn-based ethanol, then farmers will predictably react by growing more corn to meet the anticipated increase in demand. American voters are blatantly reminded of the importance of America's cornfields every four years when the race for the Presidency begins in Iowa.

Over the years, there have also been times when the government has deliberately picked winners and losers in the agricultural arena, patently

offering support for politically popular crops. Mirroring this level of government attention, it should come as no surprise that the biggest innovations
in farming and the crops that have achieved the highest yields over the past
three-decades have been one in the same. It is not a coincidence that while
yields of corn have more than doubled over the past three decades, grapefruit
growers in California have barely increased yields by 20 percent over the
same time period. As any entrepreneur will attest, innovation often follows
money and opportunity.

Today, government subsidies exert little direct influence into the decisions
Harvey makes when he decides what to plant on his farm. However, the historical pedestal the United States government has erected for growing corn
gives the crop all the advantages it needed to cement itself into American life.
These advantages have helped create an environment in which artificially
cheap corn is fueling the American food chain.

Past government support of corn is a key reason why corn-based sweeteners such as high-fructose corn syrup (HFCS) now appear in virtually all
manufactured foods, Corn Flakes included. As the price of HFCS remained
artificially low (a related sugar tariff also keeps the price of natural cane-
based sugars artificially high in the U.S.), per capita consumption of HFCS
has increased from virtually 0 lbs. in 1970 to over 73 lbs. per person in 2007,
an increase of 12,250 percent! Not all American consumers have been equally
impacted by this increase, as lower-income families consistently consume
more cheap HFCS-sweetened products than other demographics. Many
healthcare professionals believe this increase in corn-derived sweeteners is
one of the key reasons why the United States is currently facing obesity and
diabetes epidemics, both of which also disproportionately impact lower-
income families.

The statistics support this growing hypothesis of how bad farm policies
have contributed to America's healthcare crisis. For example, the real price of
fruits and vegetables increased by nearly 40 percent between 1985 and 2000,
while the cost of a soda filled with HFCS declined by 23 percent. As such, it
should be no wonder that in 2000, annual per capita consumption of sweetened sodas amounted to 440 12oz cans. In this instance, government policy
has helped create an environment where HFCS-rich soda is cheaper and more
accessible than fresh fruits and vegetables. Farmers produced approximately
600 more calories per day in 2000 as compared with 1980, yet 93 percent of
the excess calories Americans now consume as a result (approximately 300)
come from added sugars, fats and refined grains.

Reviewing the government-sponsored food pyramid that every child grows
up with, it is surprising to note that if a new food pyramid were constructed
based on what crops the government supports and what American's end up

eating, it would end up looking like the exact inverse of the actual food pyra-mid — with 440 cans of soda anchoring the base! While it is easy to imagine a Government regulator or Congressional committee looking at the recom-mended foods and then devising subsidy or support programs to make those wholesome and healthy foods more affordable and accessible to consumers, history has proven this is not the case.

Taken in sum, American farm policy has historically promoted the produc-tion of a few staple crops, notably corn. Reacting to this stable and growing supply of corn, food processers have developed ways to engineer all sorts of food products that now account for a very large percentage of America's diet. Additionally, government support of these crops has helped promote the overconsumption of corn-based foods by artificially lowering their price in the marketplace. Consumers, and especially those trying to feed a family on a budget, have responded by purchasing more foods that contain these government-supported inputs, such as Corn Flakes.

Scientists are only now starting to grapple with the consequences of this new food chain. For centuries, human bodies evolved to process specific types of foods and the nutrients they contained, and a symbiotic relationship developed between these foods and the people who ate them. This natural progression abruptly changed with the advent of the industrialized food sys-tem. Diet-related diseases are now among the leading causes of natural death in America, costing the economy upwards of $500 billion annually. This is not to say that diet-related diseases didn't exist before corn subsidies—of course they did. What has changed is the magnitude by which diets are based on processed foods and the ensuing health consequences that have resulted.

Chapter Seven

HFCS and Health

Many doctors and dietitians believe that high-fructose corn syrup (HFCS) is one of the primary culprits behind the current obesity and diabetes epidemics in America. Originally created by Japanese scientists in the late-1960s, HFCS is now found in nearly all packaged and processed foods and is especially prevalent in sweetened beverages. HFCS acts as a perfect substitute for sugar in liquid drinks, and new technology is also making HFCS a substitute for traditional sweeteners in baking and other applications that require heat. Considering that HFCS costs significantly less than natural cane-based sugars or other sweeteners, the substance has become invasively widespread.

While diet-related diseases are admittedly caused by a number of factors, the sheer rate at which obesity and diabetes have increased over the past two decades has led many experts to search for the underlying cause in this dramatic and sudden increase. Dr. George Bray, Chief of the Division of Clinical Obesity and Metabolism at the Pennington Biomedical Research Center at Louisiana State University, stated in a 2005 interview that "while genetic factors play an important role in the development of obesity . . . the rapidity with which the current epidemic of obesity has descended on the U.S . . . [suggests] environmental factors are a more likely explanation." Dr. Bray went on to state that whatever obesity's "genetic and biochemical determinants, obesity in man is susceptible to an extraordinary degree of control to social factors. Environment is very important." As this is true, Dr. Bray believes that HFCS plays a large role in these increases and that "all forms of added sugar and artificial sweeteners are bad . . . we don't need added sugar in our diet." Federal dietary guidelines recommend no more than 32 grams of sugars per day based on a 2,000-calorie diet. It is both remarkable and shocking to note that a single 20 ounce bottle of Pepsi contains nearly twice that amount.

In a seminal 2004 commentary in the American Journal of Clinical Nutrition, Dr. Bray examined how HFCS may contribute to obesity by looking at how the compound is digested by the body. Dr. Bray discovered that HFCS is digested, absorbed and metabolized differently than glucose (cane-based sugar), and that consumption of foods rich in HFCS does not stimulate insulin production in the pancreas. Insulin production is important because it signals to the brain that the body has eaten, and the absence of insulin can lead to both overeating and eating more frequently.

Other researchers, such as Peter Havel at the University of California, Davis, have also found that the fructose in HFCS is metabolized differently in the body:

> (Fructose) appears to behave more like fat with respect to the hormones involved in body weight regulation. Fructose doesn't stimulate insulin secretion. It doesn't increase leptin production or suppress production of ghrelin. That suggests the consuming a lot of fructose, like consuming too much fat, could contribute to weight gain.

According to a USDA report published in the Journal of the American College of Nutrition in 2000, fructose may also alter the balance of magnesium in the body, a deficiency which can contribute to bone loss and other health complications.

Using data from the USDA, Dr. Bray found that caloric sweeteners such as HFCS account for nearly one-sixth of the calories consumed by the average U.S. resident, and that on average, Americans over the age of two consume 132 calories of HFCS per day, while those in the top 20 percent of HFCS consumers average 216 calories. Of this HFCS, different studies hold that about two-thirds of it is consumed in beverages.

It is important to mention that added sugars are not currently required to be listed on food labels in the same way as sodium, fat or carbohydrates. Some nutritionists and health professionals have suggested that obliging food manufacturers to list the daily percentage value of added sugars in their products could encourage voluntary restraint in the consumption of those products. If the back label showed that just one soda has nearly all the sugar a person should consume in an entire day, it may encourage precisely this sort of cautionary behavior.

While food manufacturers initially began using HFCS because of its lower cost in relation to natural sweeteners, they have since found other reasons to continue using it even in the face of health concerns. For example, HFCS has been shown to irregularly extend shelf life and prevent freezer burn in packaged foods. Again, the business case for using HFCS is clear, and the absence of government incentives aligned against using HFCS in manufactured foods means that food processers will continue pumping it into any product, so long as it makes that product cheaper and more appealing to consumers.

Unfortunately, the low cost of HFCS may actually be causing some of these food manufacturers to take other actions to make additional profit. Using HFCS as a substitute for more expensive natural sweeteners decreases production costs, meaning that the ingredients needed to produce a can of soda may cost $0.16 using HFCS instead of $0.20 with cane-based sugar, a hypothetical decrease of 20 percent. Instead of decreasing the cost of that soda by 20 percent to offset these savings, manufactures may just decide to increase the size of that soda to a 20oz bottle, increasing the price to maximize revenue. A growing body of nutritionists and economists have come to this exact consensus, stating that increased package sizes in the United States are really just a ploy to keep per unit prices up. In response to these and other claims, food manufacturers and companies such as McDonald's have publicly stated that increases in package size have resulted from changing consumer preferences, though McDonalds amusingly decided to drop their "Super Size" value meal option as a result, apparently acting against these same consumer preferences.

Over the past ten years, scientists have begun to make some startling discoveries about more serious health consequences of consuming excess amounts of HFCS. Much of this research was prompted by concerned dieticians and healthcare practitioners who were noticing disturbing trends occurring in cities, towns and communities across the United States: obesity rates were growing out of control. Between 1970 and 2000, the percentage of American adults considered obese has more than doubled, rising from under 15 percent to over 30 percent. When adults who are just classified as overweight are included into this total, the percentage of Americans over the age of 20 who are classified as overweight or obese has reached a shocking high of 64 percent. Additionally, the percentage of adolescents considered overweight or obese has more than tripled during this time period, increasing from under 5 percent to over 16 percent.

The Center for Disease Control and Prevention (CDC) defines a person as overweight if their body mass index (BMI) is between 25 and 29.9, and obese if their BMI exceeds 30. BMI is a measurement between height and weight and has become the accepted way of reporting obesity statistics. According to CDC charts, a six-foot male would be considered overweight (BMI > 25) if his weight was between 184 and 221 pounds, and obese (BMI > 30) if his weight exceeded 221 pounds. While BMI is not a perfect indicator of whether or not a person is overweight – for example many athletes in peak physical shape could be considered obese based on the charts—it is the best modern measurement intended to study changes in weight.

The rapid rise in obesity rates witnessed across the country has caused some researchers and academics to postulate what could happen if the current health crisis is not reeled in. Researchers from Johns Hopkins' Bloomberg School of Public Health have stated:

> Obesity is a public health crisis. If the rate of obesity and overweight continues at this pace, by 2015, 75 percent of all adults and nearly 24 percent of U.S. children and adolescents will be overweight or obese . . . Obesity is likely to continue its increase, and if nothing is done, it will soon become the leading preventable cause of death in the United States.

Obesity's reach extends beyond America's waistlines, and a study published in the American Journal of Preventative Medicine estimates that the extra weight carried by airline passengers in the United States has increased the amount of jet fuel airlines have needed to use by over 350 million gallons in the past decade alone. Next time you are shocked at the price of a plane ticket, divert your blame away from expensive new security regulations, and instead question whether or not airlines should sell seats on the basis of weight, similar to how many airlines calculate the charges for checked bags!

The cost of obesity is also staggering, with the CDC and other sources producing estimates that place the total cost of obesity around $150 billion per year. This amount accounts for 9 percent of all healthcare expenditures in the United States, and is evenly paid for by public funds (Medicare and Medicaid) and private sources. Just as obesity forecasts continue to increase over the coming decades, the cost of treating obesity is expected to rise to over $340 billion by 2018, equating to 21 percent of total estimated healthcare costs.

This figure, and others like it, has caused some policy analysts to propose a 'fat tax' that would attempt to decrease the amount of unhealthy foods people consume by making them more expensive. According to Kelly Brownell, director of Yale University's Rudd Center for Food Policy & Obesity, a modest fat tax could also raise a significant amount of money for the government that could be used in anti-obesity campaigns. For example, a tax of just $0.01 on 12oz cans of soda could raise over $1.5 billion annually in tax revenue.

The high costs associated with treating obesity and obesity-related ailments, along with the lost economic output of an overweight and unproductive populous, have prompted speculation that obesity may very well result in a greater nutritional and health impact on the world than hunger. Along these same lines, Brownell sometimes prefaces his speeches and articles with an old Byzantine proverb that states: "He who has bread has many problems. He who has no bread has only one problem."

The overweight and obese can also act as a negative externality on healthy people in insurance pools because weight is not a consideration in health insurance premiums. Even though causal links have been drawn between obesity and healthcare costs, health policies do not charge a premium for obese people in the same way as smokers, who end up paying substantially more for healthcare. In fact, the recent healthcare bill puts in policies that outlaw some differential pricing between customers of a healthy weight and overweight or obese people. Until economic incentives are aligned so that overweight or obese Americans have to pay more for services based on their size — such as airline tickets, healthcare premiums or movie theatre seats — then prompting obese citizens to change unhealthy habits will continue to be a major challenge. Figure 7.1 illustrates the rapid increase in obesity across the U.S. from 1990-2006.

As Figure 7.1 demonstrates, obesity has increased substantially in every state over the past two decades. However, it is interesting to note that the increase in childhood obesity does not follow an even distribution and that the leanest quintile has maintained a steady average weight while the heaviest quintile has gotten significantly heavier. As will be covered in a later chapter, the economic and social mobility implications linked with this "cycle of obesity" among those at the lower end of the socioeconomic spectrum are real and severe. Also, while it is to be expected that America's aging population will naturally get heavier as it gets older, senior Americans have been hit hard by obesity, with a growing number of senior citizens being diagnosed with this severe and potentially debilitating disease.

As was mentioned in the beginning of this chapter, the extreme and sudden increase in obesity since 1970 has led a number of researchers and health professionals to view environmental causes as a key reason for its increase. Based on Figure 7.2 as well as the medical research being conducted on the health effects of HFCS, it is perhaps unsurprising that HFCS consumption and obesity rates have risen together, so closely in tandem.

Just as HFCS consumption can be tied with obesity, together, both obesity and HFCS consumption are also associated with type II diabetes — another

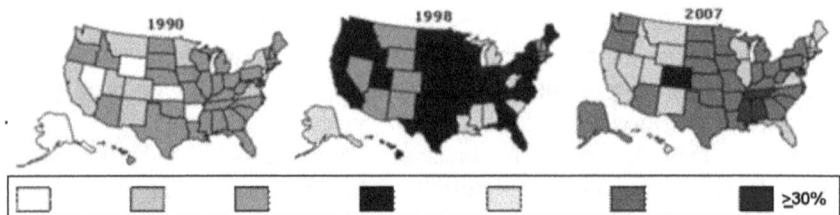

Figure 7.1. Obesity Trends among U.S. Adults.

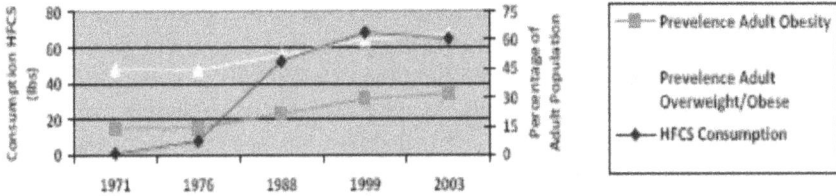

Figure 7.2.   HFCS Consumption with Overweight and Obesity.

severe, debilitating and expensive disease. About 90 percent of type II diabetes sufferers are obese, so it should be unsurprising that over the past four
decades the United States has also witnessed a staggering growth in the
prevalence of type II diabetes along with the increase in obesity. Since 1990,
the incidence of type II diabetes has risen by over 100 percent to affect over
20 million adults.

Diabetes is an incapacitating disease that affects how the human body pro-
cesses and uses food. In non-diabetic persons, the body converts energy contained in the food as it is digested into a simple sugar called glucose, which
is then used as an energy source throughout the body. No matter what type of
food is consumed, glucose is first created and then circulated into the bloodstream where it can be absorbed and used by cells as fuel. During glucose
production, a hormone called insulin is formed and secreted by the pancreas.
The amount of insulin the pancreas produces is triggered by glucose levels in
the body, and that insulin then directs the glucose from the bloodstream and
into cells to be immediately used as energy.

In diabetic persons, this process does not work properly as the body is unable to control blood sugar levels. When cells are unable to get the glucose
they need from the bloodstream, they can die. In turn, as individual cells die,
the tissues and organs they are a part of begin to degenerate until the entire
body eventually shuts down. There are different types of diabetes referred to
as type I, type II and pre-diabetes. Type I, the rarest of the three, is typically
hereditary and accounts for approximately 5-10 percent of all cases. Type
I diabetes patients are completely unable to produce insulin and depend on
synthetic means to provide their bodies with the insulin needed to stay alive.

Type II diabetes is the most prevalent form, accounting for approximately
90 of all diagnosed cases of the disease. This form used to be referred to as
adult-onset diabetes, but with the growing number of juvenile cases, the ter-
minology is being revisited. In type II diabetes, the body is able to produce
insulin, but cells become resistant to the hormone, which ultimately limits
their ability to absorb glucose from the bloodstream. This resistance period
is referred to as pre-diabetes, and at this point changes in diet or lifestyle can
reverse how insulin is being processed, thereby preventing the full onset of

type II diabetes. However, if patients do not respond and institute dietary and lifestyle changes during pre-diabetes, then the symptoms will persist until type II diabetes takes hold. By the time the disease fully sets in, the body is unable to move glucose into cells, leading blood glucose levels to become dangerously high. Historically, type II diabetes has been associated with old age, obesity, physical inactivity, race or ethnicity as well as family health history. Now this has changed, and the disease spans cultural and age-based boundaries to affect a large portion of the American population.

According to a recent report published the National Diabetes Information Clearinghouse, diabetes is the sixth leading cause of death in the United States, based on the 73,249 death certificates where it was listed as the primary cause, and another 224,000 in which it was a contributing factor. Total health care costs associated with diabetes were over $174 billion in 2007 alone, and this figure is growing rapidly.

As the years progress and the statistics become progressively more dire, the government has seen increasing pressure to take action. In the 2008 CDC Report on Diabetes, CDC director Dr. Julie Gerberding stated:

> New evidence shows that approximately 54 million people in the United States have pre-diabetes. Coupled with the nearly 21 million who already have diabetes, this places almost 24 percent of our population at risk for further complications and suffering. Together, we can and must do more to prevent this growing epidemic.

With one out of every five healthcare dollars currently spent caring for people diagnosed with diabetes, the rapid rise of diabetes and pre-diabetes has taken center stage in the healthcare debate.

Diabetes, though in most cases preventable, is a dreadful disease that can fully immobilize its victims. Complications associated with the illness include hypertension and blindness, as well as kidney and nervous system disease. Speaking to the perils of suffering from obesity and diabetes, author Greg Crister wrote in his 2004 bestseller *Fat Land* that:

> The obese diabetic may first notice strange things happening to his or her feet; they may tingle or they may become numb. When they are bruised or scratched, they may take a long time to heal. This is because excess sugar in the blood has damaged the vital nerve endings and, in the worst case, caused atherosclerosis, leading to reduced blood flow to the limbs. The consequent numbness can mask a severe injury, which can become infected, eventually leading to gangrene and amputation.

Just as with obesity, statistics are leading some doctors and dieticians to form hypotheses which link HFCS consumption and type II diabetes. Similar to the rapid increase in obesity, the United States' diabetes epidemic traces its roots back to the American diet.

Addressing this dangerous disease and its underlying causes, then, is of integral importance to improving the health of Americans. As stated in a 2004 study in the Annals of Internal Medicine, "The diabetes epidemic has already taken an extraordinary toll on the U.S. population, but the price it exacts in the future will be far greater if the current trends continue. Urgent efforts are needed to stem this tide."

At a time when two-thirds of Americans are overweight or obese, at least 25 percent of Americans suffer from metabolic diseases and over 75 million Americans have symptoms of pre-diabetes or diabetes, something needs to be done. The rapidity with which these diseases have taken hold is proof that human diets have evolved faster than human bodies and that if America's dietary patterns do not change quickly, the United States could literally be eating its way to death.

And for the record, up to 80 percent of type II diabetes can be prevented through diet and exercise.

Chapter Eight

Big Food, Meet Big Tobacco

In response to growing concerns around how HFCS may be contributing to obesity and diabetes, Big Food has launched a full-scale PR campaign combating claims that their products are causing (or even contributing to!) the epidemics. HFCSFacts.com and SweetSurprise.com are two websites the Corn Refiners Association (CRA) maintains to "dispel myths and correct inaccuracies associated with this versatile sweetener and highlight the important role high fructose corn syrup plays in our nation's foods and beverages." The CRA represents a diverse cadre of manufacturers producing HFCS, ethanol, corn oil and animal feed, in addition to many other products, and works as an interest group in sponsoring and promoting research aimed at dispelling what they see as myths or inaccuracies around HFCS and its effects on the human body.

In response to these campaigns by the CRA and numerous other interest groups sponsored by Big Food, researchers have begun to note the remarkable similarities their behavior has with previous "fact-based crusades" sponsored by Big Tobacco. Kelly Brownell, Director of Yale University's Rudd Center for Food Policy & Obesity summed up these similarities as follows:

1. *Deny your products cause harm.* In the face of considerable research showing that consumption of sugar-sweetened beverages is linked to obesity and diabetes, the president of the American Beverage Association, Susan Neely said, "Soft drinks don't play any role in the obesity epidemic." Similarly, tobacco denied harm for decades.
2. *Divert attention from your products.* The food industry states repeatedly that physical inactivity is at least the equal of food intake in promoting obesity. Inactivity is a player, but far less than previously imagined. Studies show that food intake is significantly more important than inactivity

in explaining the world spread of obesity. To burn the calories in a large fast-food meal would require the equivalent of running a marathon.

3. *Argue that government actions usurp personal freedoms.* Precisely like food companies today, tobacco companies claimed they simply offered "choice" and that they only promoted responsible consumption. As tobacco did, the food industry characterizes those who recommend government involvement with totalitarian language, calling them "nannies" and even "food fascists."

4. *Decry government action, except when it helps business.* Shouting loudly against actions such as menu labeling, calls to restrict children's marketing and taxing sugar-sweetened beverages to help recover health-care costs, the industry is silent as government subsidies provide cheap ingredients for their products. When industry is served by government action, the "nanny state" argument vanishes.

5. *Claim that education is the solution.* The industry realizes full well that government education campaigns will never have the resources to compete with industry's messages, hence industry champions education as the remedy for obesity. To offer some context, the world's largest funder of work to prevent childhood obesity is the Robert Wood Johnson Foundation, which now devotes $100m per year to the task. The food industry spends this much by January 4th of each year solely to market unhealthy food to children. What, exactly, is being marketed? Junk food. A recent report from our group at Yale found that 11 of the 15 breakfast cereals with the worst nutrition ratings are marketed heavily to children through television, the internet, or both.

In addition to these five key categories, Brownell has found other similarities between Big Food and Big Tobacco. For instance, in response to claims that traditional cigarettes were leading to lung and heart disease, the tobacco industry released "safer" versions of the products, such as the filtered cigarette. Unknowing consumers quickly jumped over to the new products as a safer alternative. Over the past year, the food industry has been taking similar steps, releasing and marketing "healthier" foods.

In 2009, PepsiCo announced a limited release of "Throwback" Pepsi and Mountain Dew that would be sweetened with natural cane based sugar rather than HFCS, which had been used in the beverages until the 1980s. In response, Dr. Pepper followed suit by releasing Dr. Pepper Heritage, also sweetened with cane sugar. Both companies have stated these new products are a result of changing consumer demand, yet neither company plans to introduce these new product lines on a permanent basis. While some food advocates believe that beverages sweetened with cane sugar are a step in the right direction, others feel Pepsi Heritage is similar to a filtered cigarette. It might have the appearance of being healthier, but so long as consumers drink more and more carbonated soft drinks over milk, water and juices, improvements in public health will still be fought incrementally.

The food industry has been vocal in wanting to avoid government intervention in the making and marketing of their products. While the notion of a government regulator determining what people can and cannot eat is a scary prospect, the government already does intervene in many (most?) industries to encourage certain types of consumer behavior. The concept at play here is known as Libertarian Paternalism and refers to when the government allows consumers to make whatever decisions they would like, while offering incentives to encourage specific, preferable types of behavior. Oftentimes, these government incentives come in the form of taxation, either through increased taxes on products the government wants people to use less of (gasoline, cigarettes, alcohol, etc.), or tax breaks for products or services that people should use more of (education, school supplies, etc.).

One of the greatest challenges in promoting government involvement in the food system is that there is no proven track record to base claims on. In many instances (such as the initial development of the USDA Food Pyramid) government action actually had the exact opposite impact than was intended. Brian Reidl, a researcher at the Heritage Foundation in Washington, D.C., remarked that "the government needs to stay out of the food system completely. Any discussion around determining and promoting healthy foods over unhealthy ones will quickly become so political that it will likely have no positive impact, and will very likely have a negative one." It is also important to remember that before any sweeping government involvement could take place, the food industry will mimic the tobacco industry in fighting legislation every step of the way.

Even with this challenge, government intervention through taxation is a proven way to influence behavior. By raising gas taxes, state governments have been able to encourage socially responsible behaviors such as carpooling or driving more fuel-economical vehicles. At the same time, people are still free to drive as much as they'd like so long as they are willing to pay for the privilege. The increased tax revenue earned through higher gas taxes can then be used to invest in roads, public transit systems, new bicycle paths or other creative ideas. Cigarettes, another example, are some of the highest taxed products in the country. While cigarette smokers are still able to purchase their product in stores across the nation, a large percentage of the tax revenue earned from each sale is then used to support government campaigns to stop smoking.

If the "fat tax" discussed in the last chapter, which could hypothetically raise over $1.5 billion in tax revenue, were applied to candy bars, fast food hamburgers, and jumbo french-fries, the amount of money available for progressive public initiatives would be unimaginable. In fact, the perennial budget deficits that have been facing the United States, coupled with rising healthcare costs across the board, have led First Lady Michelle Obama to state that obesity and diabetes are becoming threats to national security. With the deep coffers at Big Food's disposal to continue marketing unhealthy foods to unknowing consumers, any policy action that discourages the consumption of harmful processed foods through higher taxes while providing the government with a separate line of revenue to promote healthy eating could theoretically be a win-win-win, even as such a proposal would be nearly impossible to actually implement (more on this in Chapter 11 when New York's failed attempts at instituting a soda tax are addressed).

But still, critics are quick to point out accurate skepticism that any government action will end up having its intended result. Much of this criticism is related to prior government attempts to intervene in the kitchen. For example, if a person were to follow all of the government-sponsored dietary recommendations being promoted in the USDA Food Pyramid, there is a very real chance of that person getting sick and suffering from dietary disease. The primary reason why the Food Pyramid has failed to make America healthier, though, offers key lessons and insights that can and must be applied to modern day food reform.

Chapter Nine

Lessons from the Pyramid

The USDA published its first dietary recommendation report in 1894 by W.O. Atwater, the USDA's first Director of the Office of Experiment Stations. Though scientists had yet to discover specific nutritional properties for many vitamins and minerals, Atwater was an early pioneer who believed that diet exerted a major impact on health. Atwater's initial recommendations were based on the way the body could process various proportions of protein, carbohydrates and fats. As noted by USDA archives, Atwater's report "emphasized the importance of variety, proportionality, and moderation in healthful eating," continuing on to say:

> Unless care is exercised in selecting food, a diet may result which is one-sided or badly balanced. That is, one in which either protein or fuel ingredients (carbohydrate and fat) are provided in excess . . . the evils of overeating may not be felt at once, but sooner or later they are sure to appear—perhaps in an excessive amount of fatty tissue, perhaps in general debility, perhaps in actual disease.

Though Atwater was indeed ahead of his time in offering sound dietary advice, even Thomas Jefferson is known to have offered personal dietary opinions, such as his belief that American's should treat "meat more like a condiment for vegetables," by eating a diet that is predominantly plant-based.

Following Atwater's report, the USDA published its first food guide in 1916 titled "Food for Young Children." This guide divided foods into five categories: milk/meat, cereals, vegetables/fruits, fats and sugars. These recommendations advised parents to provide children with a diet that was comprised of 10 percent meat, 10 percent milk, 20 percent cereals, 30 percent vegetables/fruits, and 10 percent each for sugars and fats. Throughout the 1920s and 1930s, revised eating guides were released to provide updated nutritional recommendations for both children and adults. During the Great Depression, the USDA even sponsored eating guides to help consumers shop for foods based on their total cost so that regardless of income, Americans would know what types of foods were needed for a balanced diet.

Responding to food security concerns during World War II, President Franklin Roosevelt sponsored the National Nutrition Conference for Defense in 1941, out of which came recommended dietary allowances for different foods which would later become the National Food Guide. Over the next two decades, the USDA released numerous other dietary reports aimed at providing more precise information to American consumers about the foods they should be eating, with a specific focus directed toward vitamins and minerals as scientists conducted research revealing their various special health properties. In forming all of these dietary recommendations, environment was again important, and the USDA and the National Academy of Sciences were both careful to recommend foods that were readily available to consumers across the country. The wheat, corn and soybeans that were being produced on Harvey Sr.'s 3,000 acres of South Dakota farmland, along with the pigs and cattle the family raised, were all key inputs in the USDA's decision to recommend the daily consumption of these products.

While technological advances in South Dakota and throughout the rest of the country meant that farms were now producing more food than ever, a trip by Senators Robert Kennedy and Joseph Clark to Mississippi in 1967 led to drastic changes in America's national diet. During this field trip, the Senators witnessed emaciated children suffering from dietary diseases that were believed to only exist in third-world countries. Upon their return, CBS broadcast a special report titled *Hunger in America* that sought to raise public awareness about under-nutrition across the country. Around the same time, the USDA and the Department of Health, Education and Welfare (now known as the Department of Health and Human Services) were also noticing steep rises in rates of heart disease and stroke.

The fallout from these findings led to various Congressional inquiries that built up to the formation of the Senate Select Committee on Nutrition and Human Needs in 1968, chaired under Senator George McGovern from South Dakota. The Committee sought to both understand the diet-related diseases that were beginning to spread across the United States as well as offer prescriptive action to help curb the prevalence of dietary diseases. Under McGovern's leadership, the Committee sought to continue with the USDA's precedent of advising Americans what they should eat to help prevent the malnutrition appearing in Mississippi and elsewhere, while also advising Americans what they *should not* eat to prevent heart disease, including limiting intake of fat, saturated fat, sodium and cholesterol.

McGovern's inquiries led to the 1977 publication of the *Dietary Goals for the United States* by the Senate Select Committee on Nutrition and Human Needs. Initially the report advised Americans to curb back consumption of red meat and dairy products as a way of decreasing saturated fat and cholesterol intake. However, immediately following the publication of these findings, the meat and dairy industry lobbied a full assault on the report, leading McGovern and other members on the Senate committee to revise their recommendation to a much more subtle wording: "choose meats, poultry and fish that will reduce saturated-fat intake."

This modest change in language established a precedent for government food recommendations that stands to this day. Now, rather than offering recommendations to "eat less" of certain foods, government dietary findings revolve around "eating more" of supposedly good foods. Perhaps unsurprisingly, Senator McGovern was defeated in his next Senate election in 1980 when the large commodity and agribusiness lobbies in South Dakota rallied behind his opponent, Republican James Abnor. The lesson learned from McGovern's defeat was that any attempt to discourage Americans from eating particular types of food would be squarely met by the mighty industry lobbies.

In 1989, the popular TV show *60 Minutes* ran a piece called *A is for Apple* that discussed whether or not a little-known chemical called alar, commonly used to help apples ripen on trees, could be linked to cancer. Following the segment airing on national TV, consumer demand for the fruit plummeted, causing the apple business in Washington State and elsewhere to falter. In response to this decline, Washington State apple growers banded together and sued the show for damages, claiming that the segment defamed their product. The lawsuit was dismissed as the judge found the 60 Minutes segment targeted a particular product, and not the producers themselves. Still, the industry was not done fighting.

Shortly after the verdict was released, the *A is for Apple* ruling led the American Feed Industry to hire a team of lawyers to draft legislation that would legally prevent the defamation of any other agricultural products, holding individuals directly responsible for the loss of market resulting from comments directed toward a given commodity. The draft legislation was circulated to state legislatures, and ended up passing in thirteen states where now anyone who speaks out against the agriculture industry can be held financially liable. These "food libel" laws were brought to center stage in 1996 when Oprah remarked on her show that she was "never going to eat hamburger again" following a breakout of Mad Cow disease. Following the broadcast, cattle prices fell toward a 10-year low. Texas cattle ranchers, believing that Oprah's remarks were somehow responsible for this drop, filed a $12 million lawsuit for defamation against her to recoup losses.

Oprah ended up fighting the case and won, largely because she had the resources needed to mount an effective defense against the Texas ranchers. Even so, the cost of doing so was steep. Oprah and her team even relocated from Chicago to Amarillo, Texas, to continue filming her show during the trial. Though Oprah won, the message her case sent to the public was clear: *if you don't have anything nice to say about food, don't say it all. Even if a product is potentially harming millions of people, any public attempt to discourage its consumption could be met by legal recourse.*

The legal case against speaking negatively about particular types of food has actually helped further promote nutritionism, as lobbies and political interest groups do not exist for individual nutrients. Now, instead of honest recommendations like "eat less meat," American consumers find themselves navigating complex advice like "increase consumption of polyunsaturated fat and amino acids, while decreasing intake of cholesterol."

When the ubiquitous Food Pyramid, as seen in Figure 9.1, was first published by the USDA in 1992 it was obviously not influenced by these later court rulings, but many critics still contend that the food and agribusiness lobbies had a large role in its formation. The original Food Pyramid sought to

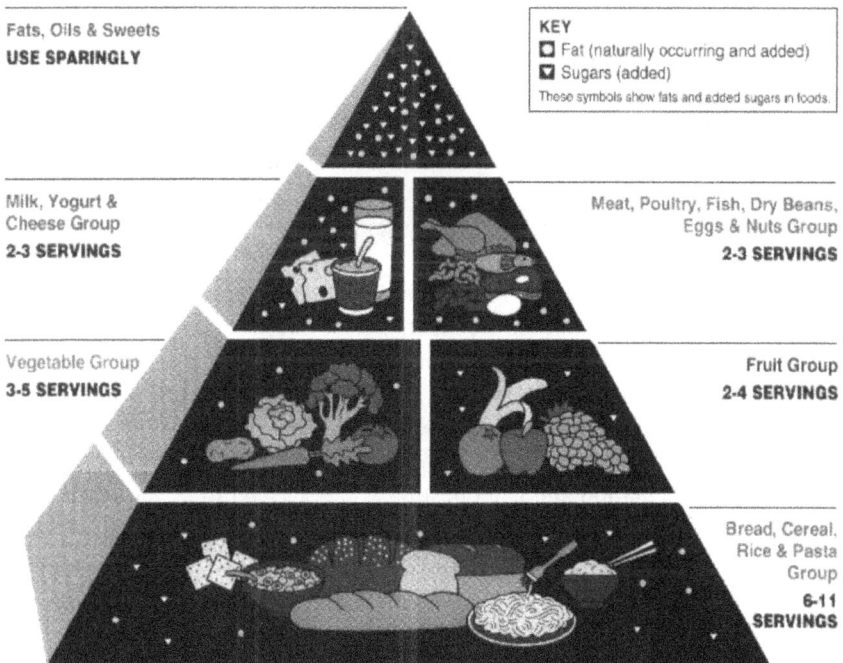

Figure 9.1.   USDA Food Pyramid, Circa 1992.

synthesize prior food classifications and provide a visual depiction of dietary recommendations.

While heavily promoted by the USDA, many health and nutrition professionals found the Food Pyramid to be problematic as it oversimplified food groups and food relationships. Responding to these critiques, in 1994 the USDA established the Center for Nutrition Policy and Promotion to "advance and promote dietary guidance for all Americans, and conduct applied research and analyses in nutrition and consumer economics," while also publishing a revised Food Pyramid.

Since being released, the Food Pyramid has been at the center of numerous controversies and debates. Many in the academic community blatantly disagreed with Food Pyramid recommendations, oftentimes believing the creation of the food pyramid was too heavily influenced by Big Food to have any credibility. Dr. Walter Willert of Harvard University Schools of Medicine and Public Health was quick to remark the USDA Food Pyramid provides "wishy-washy, scientifically unfounded advice that contributes to overweight, poor health and unnecessary early deaths."

Why all the controversy? For one, the 1992 Food Pyramid visually depicted a diet founded on grains while grouping all fats into a small category at the very top. Taking the Food Pyramid recommendations at face value, it would appear that all fats should be avoided, even though there is a huge variance in types of fats and their necessity to the human body. While saturated fats from animal protein can have negative influences on the body, unsaturated fats from nuts, olive oils, avocadoes or seafood provide a required nutrient to the body and can help to maintain healthy blood pressure, blood sugar and cholesterol levels. Comparing the fat found in bacon to the fat in a fresh avocado is like comparing the nutrients of fresh-squeezed orange juice to orange Kool-Aid.

Another problem with the Food Pyramid is that the recommendations it provides for serving quantities are inconsistent, likely because of the political pressure that was exerted influence during its creation. For instance, the Pyramid recommends a maximum of 2-3 servings per day for each of the meat and dairy categories, but a minimum of 2-4 servings for fruit. Why the USDA opted to alternate between recommended maximum and minimum servings still attracts speculation and is a question which has yet to be answered.

In determining food classifications, the creators of the Food Pyramid took simplicity to a fault. How else could it make sense to include steak, salmon, black beans, eggs, cashews and chicken in the same group? Each of these foods is vastly different and contain a varied set of nutrients, yet by including them together the USDA was essentially communicating that eating three servings of hamburger each day was the equivalent of eating a salmon filet, a handful of almonds and a serving of beans. The USDA has done little to deflect the criticism the Food Pyramid has generated.

In 2005, the Food Pyramid was updated by the Center for Nutrition Policy and Promotion to reflect changing dietary views. The Center also runs MyPyramid.org, an interactive website aimed at disseminating nutritional information and healthy eating tips. The site, a primary resource for interested consumers, has been so influenced by food lobbies and consumer groups that much of the advice it offers has been made not just worthless, but indeed damaging as it can encourage people to consume the exact foods they should be avoiding. For example, even though the negative dietary effects of consuming a diet rich in processed meats is well-documented, rather than advise consumer toward other, healthier options, MyPyramid.gov states "lower fat versions of many processed meats are available. Look on the Nutrition Facts label to choose products with less fat and saturated fat."

The revised Food Pyramid that was released in 2005 made some positive changes, such as removing images of certain foods in each category, but still is overly simplified to provide much good guidance to consumers. In updating the graphic, the USDA also turned the allocated segments into vertical

Figure 9.2.   USDA Food Pyramid, Circa 2005.

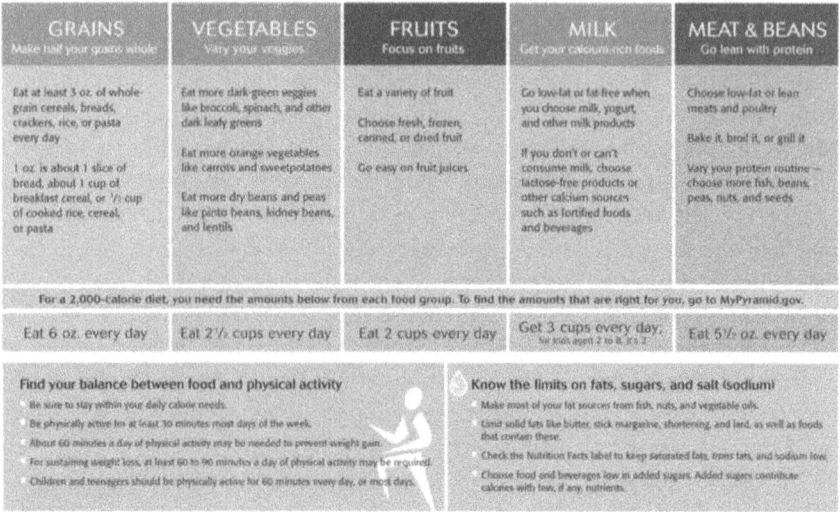

GRAINS Make half your grains whole	VEGETABLES Vary your veggies	FRUITS Focus on fruits	MILK Get your calcium-rich foods	MEAT & BEANS Go lean with protein
Eat at least 3 oz. of whole-grain cereals, breads, crackers, rice, or pasta every day 1 oz. is about 1 slice of bread, about 1 cup of breakfast cereal, or ½ cup of cooked rice, cereal, or pasta	Eat more dark-green veggies like broccoli, spinach, and other dark leafy greens Eat more orange vegetables like carrots and sweetpotatoes Eat more dry beans and peas like pinto beans, kidney beans, and lentils	Eat a variety of fruit Choose fresh, frozen, canned, or dried fruit Go easy on fruit juices	Go low-fat or fat-free when you choose milk, yogurt, and other milk products If you don't or can't consume milk, choose lactose-free products or other calcium sources such as fortified foods and beverages	Choose low-fat or lean meats and poultry Bake it, broil it, or grill it Vary your protein routine — choose more fish, beans, peas, nuts, and seeds

For a 2,000-calorie diet, you need the amounts below from each food group. To find the amounts that are right for you, go to MyPyramid.gov.

| Eat 6 oz. every day | Eat 2½ cups every day | Eat 2 cups every day | Get 3 cups every day; for kids aged 2 to 8, it's 2 | Eat 5½ oz. every day |

Find your balance between food and physical activity
- Be sure to stay within your daily calorie needs.
- Be physically active for at least 30 minutes most days of the week.
- About 60 minutes a day of physical activity may be needed to prevent weight gain.
- For sustaining weight loss, at least 60 to 90 minutes a day of physical activity may be required.
- Children and teenagers should be physically active for 60 minutes every day, or most days.

Know the limits on fats, sugars, and salt (sodium)
- Make most of your fat sources from fish, nuts, and vegetable oils.
- Limit solid fats like butter, stick margarine, shortening, and lard, as well as foods that contain these.
- Check the Nutrition Facts label to keep saturated fats, trans fats, and sodium low.
- Choose food and beverages low in added sugars. Added sugars contribute calories with few, if any, nutrients.

MyPyramid.gov

U.S. Department of Agriculture
Center for Nutrition Policy and Promotion
April 2005
CNPP-15

USDA

Figure 9.3. USDA Dietary Recommendations, 2005.

bars, as depicted in Figure 9.3, but kept the recommended serving sizes and food groups the same.

The 2005 Food Pyramid also continues with the precedent of not taking a hard stance against how foods in any given group are prepared, even those which are intensively processed. Instead, the pyramid continues to generally recommend *more* consumption, failing to emphasize the importance of fresh or whole foods above manufactured food products. The way MyPyramid.org simply refers Americans to eat more of the foods it deems nutritionally superior is problematic for a number of reasons, not least of which is the continued assertion that all meats, grains and fats are still equal.

In response to growing disillusionment with the Food Pyramid, several academic institutions have released their own dietary guidelines based on more up-to-date health knowledge. The Harvard School of Public Health recently released the Healthy Eating Pyramid, detailed in Figure 9.4, to provide competing dietary recommendations.

According to the Harvard guide, at most meals people should consume whole grain foods such as oatmeal, whole-wheat bread or brown rice. Additionally, plant oils such as olive oil, sunflower oil, canola oil or soybean oil (and yes, even corn oil!) are needed on a daily basis to provide certain nutrients and unsaturated fats. Diets should also be supplemented with 3 or more

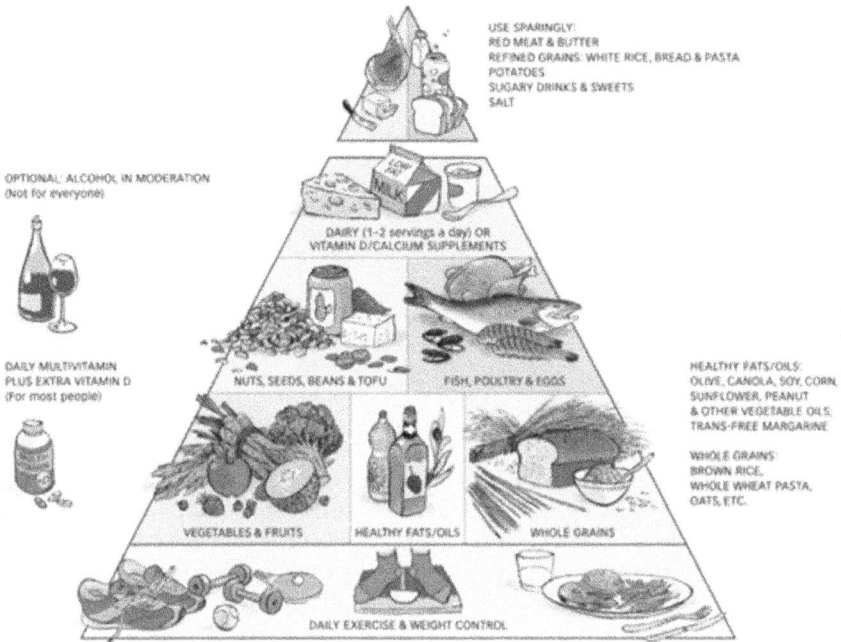

Figure 9.4.   Harvard Healthy Eating Pyramid.

servings of vegetables, 2-3 servings of fruits, 1-3 servings of nuts or legumes, 1-2 servings of dairy or calcium and 1-2 servings of poultry, fish or eggs. The Harvard guide also recommends "sparing use" of refined grains such as white rice or white bread, potatoes, pasta, sweets, red meat and butter. More holistically, the Healthy Eating Pyramid also makes concessions for alcohol based on findings that moderate consumption has proven health benefits, as well as advising people to maintain a daily exercise routine.

Not to be outdone, the University of Michigan also released their own Healing Foods Pyramid, detailed in Figure 9.5, that categorizes the foods that people should aim to consume either daily, weekly or optional (read: sparingly). The Michigan pyramid is also foundationally based in sound academic research and provides unbiased recommendations on the foods people should consume to maintain good health.

Unfortunately, although the Harvard and Michigan food pyramids provide accurate advice, their findings have been largely ignored by the general public as the USDA Food Pyramid remains the most influential source. While the USDA aims to update the Pyramid every five years, the "political realities" discussed above help prevent any drastic changes from past editions that could make or break food markets.

Figure 9.5. University of Michigan Healing Foods Pyramid.

So what can be learned from the USDA Food Pyramid? For one, any dietary recommendations that come from a government agency need to be carefully measured based on the political considerations that likely contributed to their development. While other institutions such as Harvard and Michigan have since released their own dietary guidelines, and while there are no shortage of books, magazines and TV shows dedicated to disseminating the latest dieting and eating advice, all of these sources lack both the authoritative nature of an official, government-sponsored document as well as the effective distribution channels developed by the Federal government.

In times of extreme need, such as during the Great Depression and World War II, USDA food recommendations were the authoritative source for millions of Americans as they sought to maintain a diet that would keep them fed and healthy. This precedent has been lost now as the USDA begins to grabble with an unhealthy (and unsustainable!) food supply chain that is promoted by the political weight of farm states, big agribusiness and the numerous special interest lobbies that have exerted massive amounts of money and influence into creating dietary recommendations that directly benefit their political and business interests.

Chapter Ten

The Case for Reform

As Michelle Obama's recent work on combating obesity demonstrates, the United States is now at an impasse where the nation's poor health is seriously jeopardizing the country's future. America's bad diet is the number one reason why the United States continues to get unhealthier (dietary disease is, after all, an output of diet), while hospital receipts continue to increase. Recent congressional action demonstrates that America's dietary disease is once again on the national radar, but unlike the forming of the Senate Select Committee on Nutrition and Human Needs in 1968, today's Congress has been unable to act in any constructive way. Even the landmark Patient Protection and Affordable Care Act (PPACA) that was signed into law by President Obama on March 23, 2010, falls short of addressing the fundamental problems with American health care. While the bill extends health insurance to millions of Americans by expanding Medicaid coverage and subsidizing insurance premiums, the bill misses the mark by emphasizing the treatment of disease rather than focusing on the preventable care that is needed.

In addition to the sheer cost of treating preventable dietary diseases, there are other key imperatives for reforming the American food system. For example, while obesity and diabetes are awful diseases regardless of a patient's ability to pay for treatment, proportionately, both ailments fall most on the already poor and impoverished. The reason why Americans at lower income levels suffer from higher levels of dietary disease is easy to understand considering how the food supply chain has been developed to make nutritionally poor, manufactured calories so cheap and easily available. Can a working single mother be blamed for serving her children frozen dinners that cost under $5 and require no preparation time, rather than spending the money (and time!) to make baked chicken breast with a garden salad?

Complications associated with diabetes and obesity also limit opportunities for job advancement as both diseases often result in missed work. Further, diabetic and obese parents often pass on unhealthy dietary habits that lead to obese and diabetic children, creating a "cycle of dietary disease" that in many ways mirrors the poverty cycle in America. Any policies that could contribute to obesity or diabetes can then be linked to the continuation of the poverty cycle, yet the role of diet in this pressing social issue has been largely ignored by the public, even as devoted researchers have sought to uncover why the best predictor of dietary disease in America is socio-economic status. For example, CDC data has been used to show that obesity rates for "poor" and "near-poor" people are significantly higher than for "non-poor" people.

A growing body of research has found that lower income Americans are disproportionately impacted by cheap, unhealthy food. Adam Drewnowski, a researcher at the University of Washington, has shown that many health disparities are directly linked to inequalities in income. In a seminal 2004 article looking at the causes of obesity affecting low income Americans, Drewnowski uncovered "an inverse relationship between energy density and energy cost such that energy-dense foods composed of refined grains, added sugars, or fats may represent the lowest-cost option to the consumer." For example, Drewnowski and his research team found that one dollar could buy 1,200 calories of cookies or potato chips, but only 250 calories of carrots. As poverty leads to less available income for food purchases, it should be no wonder that the Americans in most need are the ones purchasing the cheapest, and oftentimes unhealthiest, foods.

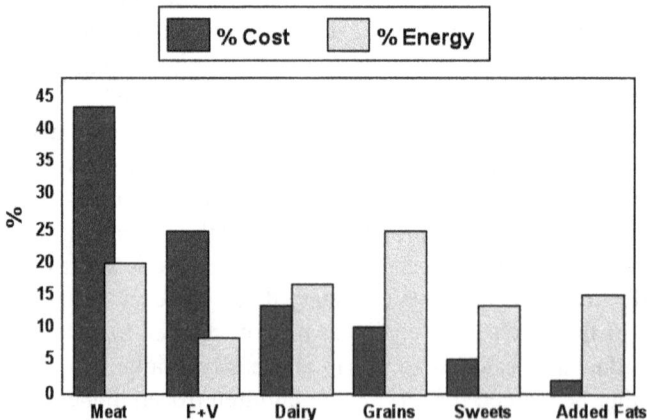

Figure 10.1. Drewnowski's Energy Density and Food Cost Comparison.

The fact that negative impacts of poor health are so disproportionately felt by low income Americans is a major social and economic issue that deserves more attention. When an entire segment of the population is unable to realize the "American Dream" because of poor health, then the entire country is in trouble. While this phenomenon should be concerning enough, the trends are actually going in the wrong direction as the discrepancy in price between healthy and unhealthy foods is growing. Between 1985 and 2000, the real price of fruits and vegetables increased by nearly 40 percent, while the cost of a HFCS-rich soft drink declined by 23 percent. As such, should be any surprise that over the past three decades, annual per capita consumption of sweetened sodas has increased over 40 percent to 440 12oz cans? However, these and other statistics which support the notion that eating unhealthy processed foods is the cheapest option do not tell the whole story.

Why is wealth the best predictor of obesity in America today? After all, for most of history it was the poor who were unable to afford food and often suffered from malnutrition. Energy dense food is cheaper than healthier fare for a number of reasons, with one of the main causes being that most energy dense food is heavily processed and contains cheap or subsidized inputs. The wonders of the American industrial food system have made it possible for consumers to spend just $2.99 for a complete frozen meal consisting of a pork cutlet, mashed potatoes, a vegetable medley of green beans and carrots and a brownie for dessert. The low cost is absolutely amazing considering that it would be difficult for a normal consumer to purchase and prepare that same meal using fresh ingredients for anywhere close to the monetary cost of a manufactured meal, which does not even account for the value of the time needed to purchase, prepare, cook and clean up after eating. *Who has time for all this?* However, while cheap food seems to be the obvious alternate to a time-consuming process like food preparation, it may not be such a blessing given the sodium, saturated and unnatural fats and undecipherable preservatives loaded into every bite.

Manufacturers in all industries know that consumers vote with their wallet, and price is the single most important driver when American grocery shoppers fill up their carts. While most consumers know that fresh eggplant, tomatoes, basil and sweet potatoes are healthy choices, it is much easier (and cheaper) to stick with calories that come from a package. Widespread misunderstanding of foods and diets, again related to the bad food recommendations promulgated by the USDA Food Pyramid, have also contributed to an environment where consumers increasingly believe they cannot afford to eat healthfully on a budget.

The obesity and diabetes epidemics are two of the most pressing issues in America today. Because of this, it is imperative that policy makers consider the implications of their actions in either contributing to or helping combat these problems. The inexpensive foods that result from overproduction of certain commodities need to be recognized as a major causal element of America's obesity epidemic. Furthermore, farm policy can and should be held responsible for creating the conditions under which these health problems have been able to thrive.

Chapter Eleven

Fixing the System

In response to the growing challenges of American agricultural and nutrition policies, certain groups across the country have begun a crusade to improve America's health. Vending machines and fast food chains are being removed from high schools, cities are banning the use of trans-fats and MSG in restaurants, food manufacturers are willingly decreasing the amount of HFCS in certain products and most importantly, American consumers are beginning to pay closer attention to the relationship between food and health.

One thing each of these efforts has in common is that they are first and foremost being driven by consumer demands and preferences. By now, it should be pretty clear that all government policies have unintended consequences. Subsidizing and insuring farmers to grow corn had intended outcomes—cheap and plentiful corn and financially secure farmers—while also contributing to unintended consequences, such as squeezing out midsized farms from the marketplace and shifting the American diet to one reliant on corn-based foods. Many of the ideas currently being floated around are tied to instituting similar government policies. For example, calls for a "soda tax" by New York Governor David Patterson failed to pick up enough momentum to turn into law. Gov. Patterson's proposal would have taxed sodas at $0.01 per ounce, raising the cost of a two-liter bottle of Coke by $0.64 or a twelve-pack by $1.44. Considering how cheaply many sodas sell for, this tax would have amounted to a price increase of anywhere from 15 to 75 percent.

Why did Gov. Patterson's soda tax fail, even as New York continues to face budgetary shortfalls that are largely linked to rising healthcare costs? For one, many New Yorkers were against using tax policy to directly influence behaviors. Ads were run by interest groups such as New Yorkers Against Unfair Taxes that said taxes should only be used to finance government programs, and that taxing a product to get consumers to use less of it was unconstitutional. National groups also involved themselves in the debate, with Susan Neely, President and CEO of the American Beverage Association saying "We understand that governments are facing tough budget challenges, but singling out one item for taxation completely misses the mark in having an effect on the national challenge of obesity."

Equally challenging was defining what a "soda" actually was. If going by sugar content (either HFCS or cane), many fruit juices, iced teas and other "non-soda" products have sugar counts in-line with many sodas. And what about diet sodas? Theoretically diet sodas would be exempt from the tax, but numerous studies have shown that drinkers of diet soda are actually un-healthier than drinkers of regular soda. If the goal was to make New Yorkers healthier, then Gov. Patterson would have to tax diet soda as well. In com-parison, the New York legislature did increase the tax on cigarettes to $1.60 per pack, citing this as an easier tax to levy as a product either has tobacco or not, a determination that cannot be made for many sweetened drinks.

Similar to calls for taxing sodas, around my home in Washington, D.C., food purchased in restaurants is taxed at 10 percent, while food purchased in a grocery store is tax exempt. While one of the goals of segmenting the tax code in this way is to encourage more people to eat and prepare foods at home, loopholes obviously exist here as well. For example, if I go purchase one doughnut from my local bakery, the donut is taxed at 10 percent, regard-less of whether or not I eat it at the bakery or take it home. But if I instead purchase one dozen donuts from this same bakery that are then sold at the Harris Teeter grocery store down the street, all twelve donuts are tax exempt.

Policies established by the USDA face similar challenges and conse-quences. For example, organizationally the USDA is structured into differ-ent components. The Farm Services Agency (FSA) is tasked with helping farmers grow food, but if these farmers want to improve their products with various "value-add" components, they are instead required to work through USDA's Rural Development office. Lack of coordinate between FSA and Rural Development has contributed to an environment where many farmers instead focus on just one end of the value chain, rather than attempt to coor-dinate initiatives and programs within the two agencies (remember the tiers of agricultural production?).

While influencing change through either government policy or USDA loan/grant programs is both complex and politically challenging, other pro-grams do exist that could have a large impact without some of the unintended consequences. Two of these ideas center on the National School Lunch Pro-gram (NSLP) and the Supplemental Nutrition Assistance Program (SNAP).

The NSLP was initially established in 1946 when President Truman signed into law a bill that provided federal assistance to meal programs operating in public and non-profit schools, as well as residential child care institutions. This bill aimed to provide "low cost or free lunches" to children at school, today providing over 30 million school children with meals each day. The USDA's Food and Nutrition Services administers the program nationally, and in order for a school lunch to be eligible for reimbursement, the meal must meet recommendations in the 1995 Dietary Guidelines for Americans which calls for no more than 30 percent of an individual's calories to come from fat (no more than 10 percent from saturated fats), while meals are also required to provide for at least one-third of the daily recommended dietary allowances of protein, Vitamins A and C, iron and calcium. Within these guidelines, schools are able to prepare their own lunches.

Unfortunately, just as nutritionism has contributed to increased dietary disease by taking nutrients out of the context of food, the school lunch requirements have also caused the focus in schools across the country to shift primarily towards meeting federal requirements, rather than on feeding children healthy and balanced meals. Additionally, as schools have sought to increase the amount of time children spend in the classroom preparing for national standardized tests that are supposed to measure their learning progress (the failure of this program as well is another great example of the unintended consequences of government policy), the time allocated for lunch and recess keeps decreasing. The result? When schools only have 20-25 minutes allocated for lunch, the foods that can be served and eaten in that timeframe are the same sorts of foods that have led to health problems with adults. Pizza, chicken nuggets, corndogs and hamburgers are all easy to prepare and fast to eat. Not so for fresh salads, soups or many pasta and rice dishes.

The reimbursement rate for school lunch programs is capped at $2.68 per meal. Again, it should be no surprise that schools, especially public schools that are constantly in a state of budgetary flux, end up selecting foods that are cheap and easy to prepare, just like pizza and corndogs. Occasionally the USDA will provide public schools with free or low-cost "premium foods," such as blueberries, asparagus or sweet potatoes, but this only happens when there is a surplus of one of these crops on the market and the USDA is required to purchase the surplus crops to keep the price at a set level. The National Sustainable Agricultural Coalition recently reported that schools witness up to a 16 percent increase in school meal participation when farm-fresh food is served, yet to-date, few schools have the means of working with these producers to provide fresh food for students.

Instilling healthy eating habits in students is one of the best ways to encourage life-long habits. To start, schools should be required to allocate at least 45 minutes of time for lunch and be provided incentives for keeping students healthy, rather than being assessed based on meeting somewhat arbitrary nutrition guidelines (a fried pork cutlet alone meets most of the current requirements). Imagine that instead of No Child Left Behind, schools received awards and recognition for having the lowest instances of dietary disease. I am almost certain that if more emphasis was places on health and the importance of maintaining a healthy lifestyle, students would enter the world much better prepared than they are now by just being able to pass a standardized test.

In addition to improving America's health by starting in schools, the Supplemental Nutrition Assistance Program (SNAP) also provides an avenue to incentivize healthy eating. Historically, SNAP was known as the Food Stamp Program and can trace its roots back to before World War II when USDA Secretary Henry Wallace established a program to bridge the divide between rural farm surpluses and urban hunger by providing people with stamps that could be used to purchase surplus crops at a discount. The program worked by marketing stamps to consumers, where for each $1.00 of food stamps purchased, they would receive a free $0.50 stamp that could be used to purchase any surplus crops. While the program began in 1939, it was phased out by 1943 as food surpluses dried up and unemployed Americans found work during the wartime economy.

In the early 1960s, the Food Stamp Program was reestablished and was again based on a model where consumers would purchase stamps, but for each purchase would receive stamps valued at an additional amount to cover the cost of food. After a brief pilot, President Lyndon Johnson called on Congress to establish a permanent Food Stamp Program, leading to the passage of The Food Stamp Act of 1964. Under the act, food stamps could be used to purchase any items other than alcoholic beverages and imported foods. In 1977 (under the guidance of Senator McGovern, amongst others), Congress reformed the Food Stamp Program to eliminate the requirement of purchasing food stamps. Now, so long as a family met eligibility criteria, they could receive free food stamps.

The Food, Conservation, and Energy Act of 2008, signed into law over President Bush's veto, revised the name of the Food Stamp Program to the Supplemental Nutrition Assistance Program (SNAP) and required benefits to now be distributed via Electronic Benefit Transfer (EBT) rather than paper stamps. Many states had already phased over to EBT, where eligible consumers received a debit card preloaded with their total benefit. The revised Act again sought to determine which foods consumers should be able to purchase with their benefit, and EBT benefits can be used to purchase any food items, other than alcohol, tobacco, non-food items (pet food, household supplies, etc.), vitamins and supplements and prepared foods or foods that will be eaten in the store. Interestingly, energy drinks with a nutrition facts label are eligible, while those that are marketed as "supplements" are not.

Under these guidelines, a packaged deli sandwich from a super market is ineligible, but a purchase of bread, meat and cheese is eligible. Of course, interpretation of this rule has also had unintended consequences. As many SNAP recipients lack the means, motivation or knowledge to cook wholesome meals, frozen pizzas, hotdogs and packaged foods are more likely to be purchased than fresh foods that require preparation prior to eating. Resulting from these rules, grocers, and especially those in urban areas where shelf space comes at a higher premium, end up stocking their shelves with the foods that sell best. Considering that nearly 40 million Americans rely on SNAP, it should come up as no surprise that their preferences, and the foods their benefits are eligible to purchase, end up lining shelves across the country.

Fortunately, there are options to fix this system. As mentioned earlier, people at the lower end of the economic spectrum (and thus more likely to receive SNAP benefits) are often more unhealthy than other consumers. The USDA's SNAP website already claims the program "helps put healthy food on the table," so why not build in requirements to ensure the foods actually being purchased are in fact healthy? While this sort of proposal will surely attract vocal opponents who will claim that the government is "forcing SNAP recipients to buy certain foods, or else go hungry," the fact this is an existing government benefit, and not a new tax proposal, will certainly make it more palatable. As purchases made via EBT can be easily tracked (think about your monthly credit card statement that shows you the breakdown of how much money is spent each month for food, entertainment, gas, etc.), a starting point for this plan could be to look at what foods SNAP recipients are actually purchasing.

If, as I suspect, the by-and-large majority of SNAP funds are spent on unhealthy, processed and prepared foods, then that data will hopefully find traction in the halls of Congress and lead to new purchasing requirements, such as requiring 20 percent of each EBT to be used for fruits and vegetables. SNAP recipients will have no choice but to start eating more healthy foods. An ancillary benefit of allocating a certain percentage of each EBT towards fruits and vegetables is that demand will automatically increase for these products across the country, and especially in small, urban grocers. As stores begin to respond to consumer demands and stock more foods that meet the new 20 percent fruit/vegetable requirement, other consumers not receiving SNAP benefits will then be exposed to an increase in these foods each time they buy groceries. While opponents of such a plan are sure to come up with creative ways to communicate why this is a bad deal for consumers ("the government is deciding for you what you can or can't eat!"), it is also a clear proposal to improve health across America, and especially for those at the bottom of our food system.

Chapter Twelve

Local, Regional, National

It comes as no surprise that agriculture production across the United States is split between small, medium and large producers. While there has been a recent increase in the number of small, niche farms along with giant, industrial operations, mid-sized "family farms" have struggled to keep pace. Small farms, especially those close to urban areas, have benefited recently from an increase in urban farmer's markets where they are able to sell their products at a steep premium to conscientious consumers. On the other end of the spectrum, continued consolidation amongst farms in the Midwest, particularly those growing row crops, has squeezed out mid-sized farms as they have been unable to keep pace with the technological investments that have increased productivity for corn, wheat and soy. Consolidation has also occurred in livestock, as many farmers have followed Harvey's example in focusing on their competitive advantage in row crops, also opting out of making substantial investments in infrastructure to comply with USDA and EPA livestock rules.

As we look towards a 21st Century Agricultural System, what does the division look like between local, regional and national producers? When determining how each of these players fits into a this system, it is important to recognize that the goal of the 21st Century Agricultural System is to ensure a food supply that is healthy, cheap and secure, while also promoting diversification amongst producers to both mitigate production risk and ensure consumers have access to the foods they want. Coupled with these tenets, the 21st Century Agricultural System also needs to benefit farmers and those who are involved with food production throughout the supply chain to ensure they are recognized and rewarded for their efforts in keeping the country fed, whether they own a giant industrial farm, run a network of farmer's markets or manage food supply for a school district.

In establishing such a food system, there is a need for local, regional and national agriculture operations to produce food and respond to consumer preferences. The growth in small and large farms over the past decade has been great in helping stock farmers markets and keep commodity prices low, but the lack of mid-sized agriculture has had real and far-reaching implications. When looking at the environmental impact of food production, I mentioned earlier that only one percent of food is produced and consumed within a 200 mile radius, and that agricultural production is responsible for around 20 percent of total fossil fuel use in the America. Many people interpret this statistic to mean that more food should be grown and distributed locally to decrease fossil fuel use. Perhaps somewhat surprisingly, the efficiencies of industrial agriculture are such that an apple grown in Washington State and purchased at my local grocer in D.C. probably has a smaller carbon footprint than one grown in nearby Virginia and driven in on the back of a pickup truck to be sold at a farmers market. While the consolidation on Harvey's farm has meant that he no longer raises cattle or hogs, or grows oats and barley, his farm is a great example of how focusing on competitive advantages is needed for farmers, both to feed the country and to make ends meet.

While parts of this book may appear to be somewhat critical of large-scale industrial agriculture, there is a very important place for these producers in the 21st Century Agricultural System. The focus of these producers on growing row crops and efficiently providing commodity foods to processers and manufactures is absolutely critical in keeping the country fed while maintaining low food prices. America needs corn from Iowa and South Dakota. Similarly, California and Florida's giant orange, strawberry and tomato growers need to continue expanding output to meet our country's demand for these crops. While there will always be areas for improvement, such as making sure soil nutrients are replenished when growing monocultures and ensuring responsible use of genetically modified seeds (GMOs) and fertilizers, agricultural production will continued to be dominated by large-scale producers.

Small producers will also maintain their position in the 21st Century Agricultural System. Consumers, and especially wealthy households in urban areas, place a high value on locally produced foods and the ability to purchase deliciously fresh foods at farmer's markets. Small farms provide needed diversification in the food system. In addition to supporting the local communities they operate in, many small farms have also led the charge into producing organic products, developing their own best practices for organic production that can later be picked up by industrial producers. Small farms are also typically good stewards of their land with many adhering to tried-and-true farming practices that limit pesticide and fertilizer use, while also avoiding the use of GMOs.

Now what about mid-sized farms? As small farms have continued focusing on their immediate geography (many of the farms located in rural Virginia and Maryland target Baltimore and Washington, D.C. to sell their crops), and large farms have continued the march towards consolidation by focusing on national supply and demand trends, mid-sized farms have been forced to fight for survival between these two ends of the spectrum. Looking towards the 21st Century Food System, expanding the role of these producers is absolutely critical. While mid-sized farms are too small to compete in basic commodities—corn, soybeans, hogs and cattle—they are well-positioned to benefit by scaling profitable niche markets (the same ones small/local farms focus on). Similar to how consolidation amongst large farms has improved the efficiency of their supply chains, mid-sized or regional farms can form cooperatives with other farms, benefiting from these partnerships in growing, marketing and selling their food. In doing this, mid-sized farms are able to form diversified cooperatives that provided needed competition in the marketplace, providing consumers with an option that falls in between mass-produced commodity foods and going to the farmer's market each weekend to buy lettuce. These operations are now referred to as regional food networks or "agriculture-of-the-middle." Regional food networks are supported by farms that are not big enough to successfully grow and market bulk commodities, or sell food directly to consumers.

One of the best examples of a successful regional food network is Good Natured Family Farms (GNFF), an alliance of over 100 family farms around Kansas City who produce and market all-natural meat (beef, chicken, turkey, bison), local honey, dairy (cheese, eggs, milk), and local farm fresh fruits and vegetables. GNFF requires their members to adhere to natural and organic production methods, but in return for this commitment, producers benefit from GNFF's sales network around Kansas and Missouri, selling foods directly in some of the largest grocers in Kansas City, such as Hen House Markets, Balls Price Choppers as well as the Community Mercantile in Lawrence, Kansas. Consumers willingly pay more for the diverse foods being produced by GNFF, as they associate the GNFF seal to mean their purchase will support a local farmer who adhered to the highest standards in producing their food.

Next door to GNFF in Kansas City, the Good Food Good Futures (GFGF) alliance is also working to promote regional agricultural systems. GFGF began as an initiative of the American Royal Association, a "110-year-old civic organization focused on promoting American agriculture education and agrarian values," and also the namesake of the Kansas City Royals major league baseball team. GFGF is comprised of a diverse group of stakeholders from around the Kansas City region who have banded together to explore how agriculture production, food retailing, information technology, health-care providers and government agencies can work together to promote mid-sized farms. GFGF is working with GNFF to help increase access to fresh, local food in urban Kansas City, and has also worked with school systems and employers to help encourage them to include healthier and regionally produced food into their meal plans. By improving access to healthy food from local farms, GFGF is helping address their community's health, while supporting local farmers in the process.

Recently, the USDA introduced the "Know Your Farmer Know Your Food" initiative that is also aimed at promoting local and regional farms. Know Your Farmer Know Your Food is a USDA-wide effort to "create new economic opportunities by better connecting consumers with local producers. It is also the start of a national conversation about the importance of under-standing where your food comes from and how it gets to your plate." This ini-tiative provides grants and resources to help midsized farms grow and market their products with the goals of supporting local farmers, strengthening rural communities, promoting healthy eating and protecting natural resources.

In practice, Know Your Farmer Know Your Food is working to scale the same model that Good Natured Family Farms has pioneered in Kansas City. By providing farmers with the training and resources to better produce and market their crops, Know Your Farmer Know Your Food is helping meet consumer demand for fresh, local food while also ensuring all products meet USDA safety standards. Largely thanks to these two programs, a national movement is now underway that promises to increase the availability of local food in communities across the country, providing consumers with options to complement their diet with fresh and healthy food, while supporting a whole new cadre of farmers and producers.

Chapter Thirteen

Getting It Right at W&M

After graduating from high school in the suburbs of Washington, D.C. in 2008, Jane Gray decided to take a gap year before enrolling in college to gain real-world experience and further hone her interests into a field of study. After looking across the country for innovative living models, Jane was drawn to Portland, Oregon. Moving to Portland meant leaving behind her family and friends and starting her own life away from the suburbia that had marked her childhood. Two weeks before moving, Jane was still searching for jobs in the Portland area when a chance encounter in a Washington-area Whole Foods led to an offer to work at a sustainable architecture and eco-cultural restoration firm in Portland.

On the west coast, it quickly became obvious that an alternative, more creative approach to the world was possible—a far cry from the type of thinking Jane grew up with in Northern Virginia. As Jane learned more about architecture and the principles of design, she realized that nothing works in isolation. Just as a building is greater than the sum of its parts, the complex ecosystem that supported Portland's food system extended far beyond supermarket shelves. Soon, Jane was immersed in studying just how food systems work, examining in detail the connections between the food a community eats and its economic, environmental and social viability. After six months at the design firm, Jane was presented an opportunity to work as a councilmember for City Repair, a non-profit that helped her to understand how food could become a medium to connect and strengthen communities. Gradually, Jane began to recognize just how crucial a healthy food supply is for supporting a dynamic community.

By the time Jane returned to the East Coast after her year in Portland, she had decided on enrolling at the College of William and Mary in Williamsburg, VA, the country's second oldest college. Jane was excited to start her academic career at the College, and was particularly enthused to see how she could apply some of the principles she had learned in Portland to her new life back home by taking advantage of a new academic initiative at William and Mary that would allow her to design her own major and curriculum over Sustainable Systems.

However, when Jane arrived in Williamsburg in the fall of 2009, excitement turned to disillusionment as she experienced firsthand the inner workings of the industrial food system. In college, the dormitory Jane moved into was not well-equipped for cooking, so like millions of other college students across the country, Jane ended up purchasing one of the required school meal plans. Under this plan, Jane was now entitled to consume buffet-style meals three times per day at cafeterias across campus. It was not long before Jane became dissatisfied with the lack of variety and mass of unhealthy, processed foods available in this program, which led her to kick-start a campaign to improve local and fresh offerings at the school cafeterias.

To Jane, the College's potential for creating a self-sustaining food system on both an individual and institutional level seemed enormous. Given that William and Mary has long-sought to establish the College as an ecologically forward-looking institution, Jane turned out to be in the right place. The school maintains an official College Sustainability Policy with a Committee on Sustainability (CoS) that links students, faculty and staff together in developing strategies to make the school more sustainable. The CoS maintains the power to allocate grant money to fund sustainable initiatives on campus, which have included the installation of a storm water management rain garden that mitigates heavy erosion as well as a research project which delved into the inner-workings of the local food network. This grant money is collected annually from students who support the effort by paying a $15 "Green Fee" each semester. The growth in participation and student interest has been enormous since the committee's inception, reflecting an avid interest at all levels in exploring alternative solutions to current, unsustainable practices.

The success of the College's one-year old compost program, which diverts 100 percent of organic wastes from school cafeterias to a nearby biofuel processing plant, had already profoundly impacted both the school and surrounding community. William and Mary's success at composting leftover food rather than sending it to the landfill has become a model for the surrounding region, and the school is now helping establish similar composting programs for both small-scale residential and mid-sized commercial companies. While Jane's first objective in bringing locally produced food to campus was to improve student health through improved access to healthy food, she also hoped to use this influence to encourage the surrounding area to adopt more sustainable agricultural policies.

As Jane began building her case for improving access to local food on campus, she started running into resistance. To start, the same global distribution methods that helped guide Harvey into row crops and away from some of the crops his father grew impaired access to local foods. Around Williamsburg, the local, small-scale farmers were struggling in a hostile market where production costs heavily outweighed the price of industrially-produced food. This phenomenon was especially true for the growing cadre of organic farmers, as abstaining from pesticide and herbicide use makes predicting a regular harvest difficult, to say the least.

As with breaking into any new industry, Jane encountered barriers when trying to alter the existing food business practices of the College and integrating into the existing local food economy. Unfortunately for Jane, William and Mary was still reeling from the recession by instituting budgetary cuts across the ledger. While many administrators agreed that supporting local producers and businesses would both invigorate the area economy and make Williamsburg an even more attractive place to live and attend school, school administrators kept going back to the bottom-line, maintaining the school could not afford to spend more on sourcing food. Another barrier Jane encountered was a wall of school liability laws that required any vendor providing food to the College to have at least $4 million in liability insurance coverage, a clearly prohibitive barrier to small-scale or even mid-sized farming operations. To conform to this rule, the College would hire sourcing companies with liability coverage (recall the third or fourth tiers of agriculture production) to act as the liaison between farms and the cafeteria.

Jane recognized that forming key partnerships with these agriculture sourcing companies would continue to be critically important as maintaining a steady supply of food from small- and mid-sized producers would be virtually impossible given the volume of campus demand. The mass quantity and regularity required for the College mandated procurement systems that could meet the demand. Like in Groton, SD, most of the production around Williamsburg had shifted to row crops like soy, wheat and corn, which means that procuring food from local farms around Williamsburg would limit the variety of food available for purchase.

Still, Jane was not disheartened. Looking at rival institution Washington and Lee University (W&L) in Lexington, VA, Jane saw an approach that could work for her school. W&L had pioneered a new method of sourcing local foods by waiving the unreachable requirements of liability insurance and production guarantees, opting instead to hire employees of the college to personally inspect local farms and gauge their operations against two national standards: the USDA Good Agriculture Practices guidelines and the Food Alliance certification. If a local farm meets these requirements, W&L is able to contract directly with the farm to source food. The case of W&L provided a particularly shining example to Jane, as William and Mary does not manage its own operations but is contracted to Aramark—a large-scale food distribution company which is inimitably matched to college-scale clientele. Aramark procures most of William and Mary's fresh food through Baker Brothers, a Virginia-local produce distributor, whereas W&L openly partnered with Cavalier Produce, another local produce distributor which only requires $1 million in liability insurance. Seemingly small decisions like these add up in a big way toward securing a sustainable future for food procurement, especially when they supply the hefty demands of higher education.

After approaching the college's Aramark representative directly, Jane was offered the position of Sustainability Intern for Dining Services along with a few other select students. Together, they worked with the head chefs of Dining Services to develop a menu that reflected seasonal changes in produce availability (in Japan, it is a required course for students to build a menu in which nutritional needs are balanced. This is the government's way of trying to educate kids and combat the rise of malnutrition/obesity). Through this initiative, Jane and the other interns helped to design a matrix that overlaps the College's academic calendar with produce availability such that during summer programs, students are provided with fruits, berries and tomatoes, while root vegetables and lettuce appear more prominently on campus during the transition into fall. To complement these modest menu changes, Jane is working on developing an education and outreach campaign to further instill the values of the local food movement across the College and Williamsburg.

On campus, Jane led an effort to establish a robust herb garden — the basil, rosemary, thyme and other herbs produced in the garden are now fed to students across the campus dining program, as well as to the broader community as part of the Campus Kitchens program that provides meals to low-income families around Williamsburg. In promoting the garden across campus, Jane is helping students, faculty and staff connect on a higher level with the food they eat, facilitating an understanding of the broader relationships that exist in our ecosystem. The gardens she helped to create embody the concept of localization from construction to planting—even the seedlings were purchased at the Williamsburg Farmer's Market—and also provide another outlet for the compost that is being formed each year. By gathering herbs from outside the cafeteria's doors, it is projected the school will save between $4-6 per 4 oz. bundle of herbs, equaling up to a few thousand dollars per year.

In addition to working within the school's systems of food procurement and on-site gardening, Jane saw the value in reaching even further to work in the greater community while providing students a viable alternative to campus dining menus. Working toward this goal, she became a manager of the student-run food co-op, the RealFood Williamsburg Community Cooperative, which received its official 501(c)(4) nonprofit status in 2010. The cooperative functions year-round, offering produce, dry goods, meats, dairy and deli items to both students and those in the community who hold a membership. At prices significantly below those found at the local farmer's market, RealFood functions to make wholesome food accessible to students and Williamsburg residents alike. Jane and the other cooperative managers also work hard to facilitate ongoing workshops which allow neighbors to empower each other to actively engage in growing, preparing and understanding their food more holistically.

Jane provides just one example of a student working to improve both campus and community health by promoting the healthy sustainable food movement. Colleges and universities like William & Mary and Washington & Lee are well positioned to take a leadership role in promoting a 21st Century Food System, and as Jane prepares to spend the next three years on campus finishing out her major, she plans on dedicating even more time to making her ideas actionable.

Chapter Fourteen

Summary and Conclusion

Due to government programs and the amazing efficiency of U.S. farmers, American's spend less on food than any other industrial nation in the world, yet also suffer from some of the highest rates of dietary disease. The United States has proven that it is possible to be overfed and undernourished. While there will always be a certain segment of the population in any country who go to bed hungry at night, the Supplemental Nutrition Assistance Program (SNAP) and the National School Lunch Program (NSLP) have largely alleviated traditional hunger, even as these programs have also failed to make the people the most in need of good nutrition healthier. With American farmers expanding output year on year, a natural consolidation has occurred in the farm industry that has squeezed out midsized farms and increased the purchasing power of large farms and agribusinesses. Agriculture consolidation changed food supply chains, to the point where food is treated like any other commodity, produced and shipped around the world, keeping Americans (and the world at-large) fed, while also leading to environmental degradation.

Within each of these challenges, opportunities do exist. To complement the extraordinary output of industrial agriculture operations, the USDA should do more to support midsized farms. While midsized farms will never compete with large (10,000 acre plus) operations in growing row crops, they do have an important place in the market to provide fresh foods to consumers across the country. Midsized farms can also successful form cooperatives, such as Good Natured Family Farms in Kansas City, to further increase their reach and ability to market and sell foods to consumers. Small farms will continue to fill their niche as well, providing high-end foods to demanding consumers, while also ensuring the United States maintains a diverse food supply.

Both SNAP and NSLP provide a starting point for government policy makers to begin addressing some of the inequities in U.S. agriculture that have led to a system where people at the lowest ends of the socioeconomic spectrum are also those who are most unhealthy. By using SNAP and NSLP to increase the amount of healthy food available to these households, the government could greatly improve health prospects for this demographic, improving their standard of living and further combat the cycle of poverty that continues to limit opportunities for those in most need.

In researching and writing this book, I became both encouraged and disillusioned at the state of American agriculture. It really is amazing that so few people are able to effectively feed so many, and that innovations in rural America continue to increase crop yields and allow for further diversification in the economy. The many organizations working towards improving access to healthy foods, such as the cities, school districts, not-for-profits and interest groups (such as Good Food Good Futures) are moving the ball in the right direction and will hopefully continue to play an important role in improving America's health. Even with the encouraging work done by these organizations, the unwillingness by politicians and American consumers to recognize tradeoffs and the connection between food and health has been disheartening, to say the least.

A few themes hopefully resonated throughout this book. For one, unintended consequences apply to most farm and food programs, and as a result of many of these consequences, the United States has both the best and worst worlds when it comes to agriculture. As I was researching and writing this book, I found the connection between farm policy, agricultural output and health and nutrition was not nearly as simple or straightforward as I had naively assumed. If anything, the sheer complexity of U.S. agriculture should provide reason for us to step back and re-evaluate how the sector works so that we may better understand the connection between what we grow, the foods we eat and the impact that food has on our bodily health.

In the end, the relationship between health and agriculture comes down to personal preferences and choices. Regardless of whether or not government policy makes corn more available than asparagus, the majority of consumers have access to healthy foods and the decision to eat healthy is ultimately up each one of us. While there are actions the government, producers, marketers and food retailers can and should take to increase availability of healthy foods and encourage good eating habits, the decision to be healthy will remain yours.

To help combat the myth that healthy food is expensive and takes a lot of time to prepare, a listing of recipes is included in the appendix that can serve as a guide for your next trip to the grocery store. Many healthy meals can be prepared for under $10 and in less than 10 minutes, and should you start cooking with these ingredients, I can guarantee healthy eating becomes contagious.

Good luck, and enjoy!

Appendix

Quick Tips for Healthy Eating

With all of the colorful boxes and displays that direct consumers towards packaged and processed foods in grocery stores across the country, it can be pretty easy to lose sight of the whole foods that are often quarantined to just one corner of the store. While a whole apple or tomato might not come in a box with catchy labels—"*low fat!*" or *"½ the calories!"*—a multitude of healthy meals can be cooked cheaply and quickly using these ingredients. Cooking with whole foods is a great way to start understanding the connection between food and health, and while most whole foods don't come with cooking instructions, oftentimes preparing delicious meals with these products takes less time than making a frozen pizza.

10 FOODS TO KEEP AROUND

The following ten foods are great staples that should be in every kitchen. These foods "play well with others," and are all you need to complement or spice up pastas, salads, steak/seafood/chicken and many other dishes. Many of these foods are used in the below recipes, and they are also great on their own—go ahead, give them a try!

1. Carrots
2. Tomatoes
3. Eggs
4. Sweet Potatoes
5. Eggplant
6. Walnuts
7. Olive Oil

8. Grapefruit
9. Lemon
10. Quinoa

10 MEALS IN 10 MINUTES FOR UNDER $10

Eating healthy doesn't have to be expensive or time consuming. With the above staple ingredients stocked in your kitchen, adding a few additional ingredients can make for delicious and well-rounded meals. Here are 10 to try, all of which cost under $10 per meal and can usually be prepared in under 10 minutes (*note: 10 minutes is calculated based on total preparation time, not cooking time*):

1. Summer Salad
2. Middle East Eggplant
3. Quinoa with Vegetables
4. Quick and Healthy Pasta
5. Baked Sweet Potato Fries
6. Grandma Clare's Chili
7. Not Your School Lunch Pork Cutlets
8. Veggies and Eggs
9. Avocado and Grapefruit Salad
10. Eggplant Parmesan
Bonus: Grilled Corn on the Cob

1. Summer Salad

This salad is great at all times of the year, but the citrus flavors are particularly refreshing during summer. Add a salmon filet (blackened, baked or pan-fried) to turn this into a meal.
Ingredients:

- 1 head of Romaine lettuce (can be substituted with any other leafy green, such as spinach or arugula)
- 2 Tomatoes
- ½ Grapefruit
- Handful of Walnuts
- Olive Oil
- ½ Lemon

Directions: rinse and chop lettuce, added diced tomatoes and ½ grapefruit (just spoon out the sections of fruit), toss in a handful of walnuts, then make a dressing out of 3 Tbs. Olive Oil and ½ Lemon. Salt and pepper to taste.

2. Middle East Eggplant

This eggplant salad is delicious and can be served either cold or hot. It also stays well in the fridge for up to five days, so make a batch then add it as a spread to sandwiches throughout the week, a dip for pita chips or a standalone appetizer.
Ingredients:

- 1 medium-sized eggplant
- 3 Tomatoes
- ½ Onion (can be red, yellow, Vidalia)
- Olive Oil
- ½ Lemon
- 1 clove Garlic
- 2 Carrots
- 1 Handful Parsley, Dill, Basil or Cilantro (optional)

Directions: halve eggplant, sprinkling each open side with salt and then dabbing with a paper towel to remove any bitterness. Place eggplant on deep plate with about ¼ cup of water added to the base, microwaving for about 5 minutes. Remove, cover and let sit for a minute, then return to microwave for another 3 minutes. Once cooled, spoon out eggplant into large bowl and mix with diced tomatoes, onions, carrots, minced garlic and any herbs (optional). Add juice from ½ lemon and ¼ cup olive oil, adding salt and pepper to taste.

3. Quinoa with Vegetables

Quinoa is one of the best foods most people don't know about. This versatile grain can be purchased at many grocery stores across the country, typically for under $2 per box. Quinoa is like a South American version of couscous, and is the only grain that contains all of the essential Amino Acids, leading the Incas to refer to it as "mother grain."
Ingredients:

- 1 cup quinoa
- 2 Tomatoes

- ½ Squash or Zucchini
- ½ Onion (can be red, yellow, Vidalia)
- Olive Oil
- 1 Lemon
- 1 clove Garlic
- 2 Carrots
- 1 handful Parsley, Dill, Basil or Cilantro (optional)

Directions: rinse quinoa thoroughly under cold water, then add to a saucepan with a ratio of two parts water for each one part quinoa (for each cup of quinoa, add two cups of water), add diced onion and squash or zucchini, shredded or diced carrots, and 1 clove of minced garlic. Bring water to a boil, and then reduce to simmer, covering quinoa until all water is absorbed and the grain looks translucent. Next, add in juice from one lemon, a few dashes of olive oil, diced tomatoes and salt/pepper to taste. If you have herbs such as parsley, dill, basil or cilantro, chop it and add in as well!

4. Quick and Healthy Pasta

Pasta is easy, cheap, fast and eating it just makes people happy. For this dish, combining fresh vegetables, cheese and nuts makes for a delicious and well-rounded meal, while adding optional herbs or chicken adds an extra dose flavor or protein. Go ahead, enjoy hot or cold!
Ingredients:

- 1 box angel hair pasta (regular or whole wheat)
- 2 Tomatoes
- Olive Oil
- 2 Carrots
- ¾ cup parmesan cheese
- 1 handful Walnuts
- 1 handful Basil or Cilantro (optional)

Directions: cook one package of angel hair pasta in salted, boiling water, according to package directions. Drain, then toss with ¼ cup olive oil and ¾ cup of freshly grated parmesan cheese. Add diced tomatoes, shredded carrots and halved walnuts. Complementing this dish with chopped basil or cilantro adds a refreshing kick! Also, adding in grilled or pan-fried chicken turns this dish from light and airy to hearty and filling.

5. Baked Sweet Potato Fries

Sweet potatoes are stocked full of potassium, fiber, folate, and Vitamins A and C, and are delicious whether baked, fried or grilled. Sweet potatoes also have a long shelf-life (just store in a cool, dry place), making them perfect for year-round enjoyment.
Ingredients:

- 2 Sweet Potatoes
- Olive Oil
- Salt, Pepper
- Onion (optional)
- Garlic (optional)

Directions: julienne 2 sweet potatoes, tossing with olive oil and sprinkling with salt and pepper. Place on a baking sheet and bake at 400 degrees for 20-25 minutes, turning occasionally until done. If your significant other doesn't mind, add diced onion and minced garlic for extra flavor!

6. Grandma Clare's Chili

Chili is versatile, filling and down-right delicious. This recipe combines fresh and canned ingredients to deliver a nutritious meal in no time.
Ingredients:

- 2lbs Ground Turkey
- Olive Oil
- 2 Onions
- 2 Cloves Garlic
- 4 Tomatoes
- 4 Carrots
- 2 Cans Black Beans
- ½ cup Parmesan Cheese
- 1½ tsp chili powder
- 1½ tsp salt/pepper

Directions: brown turkey with onions and garlic on stove top, using Olive Oil to coat pan. Drain, and then add remaining ingredients, dicing all vegetables and simmer for 10 minutes. Top with grated parmesan cheese and serve with whole wheat tortillas.

7. Not Your School Lunch Pork Cutlets

OK, so with the National School Lunch Program phasing out their pork cutlets for additional servings of fruits and vegetables (maybe someday?), start making healthy pork cutlets at home.
Ingredients:

- 1lb. thinly-sliced Pork Cutlets
- 2 Cloves Garlic
- 4 Tomatoes
- ½ cup Breadcrumbs
- ¼ cup of freshly grated Parmesan Cheese
- 1 Egg
- Olive Oil
- Salt/Pepper to taste

Directions: mince garlic and add with breadcrumbs and cheese. Then, lightly beat egg and place in pan, dipping cutlets into egg and then covering them with breadcrumb mixture. Heat about 3tbs. Olive Oil in a sauté pan, pan frying each cutlet for about 3-5 minutes per side. After finishing, pan fry sliced tomatoes in same pan, adding additional olive oil, salt and pepper to taste.

8. Veggies and Eggs

Omelets and scrambled eggs are delicious and are perfect to be enjoyed at any time of the day. Serve with baked Sweet Potato Fries and a ½ Grapefruit for a balanced meal, whether for breakfast or dinner.
Ingredients (per scramble):

- 3 Eggs
- 1 Tomato
- ¼ Green or Red Pepper
- Handful of fresh Spinach
- Handful of fresh Basil
- Olive Oil
- Salt/Pepper to taste

Directions: lightly beat eggs in a bowl, adding diced tomato and green or red pepper. Heat up frying pan with 1tbs. Olive Oil on medium heat. Add egg mixture, stirring occasionally. After eggs begin cooking, add chopped basil and spinach. Once eggs are no longer runny, remove, season with salt and pepper, and enjoy!

9. Avocado and Grapefruit Salad

When avocados are in season, they can often be purchased for around $1 each. This salad brings out the best flavors in both avocado and grapefruit for a nutritious and easy lunch.
Ingredients:

- 3 Avocados
- 1 Grapefruit
- 1 Lemon
- Olive Oil
- 1tbs Dijon Mustard
- Salt/Pepper to taste

Directions: create a vinaigrette dressing by combining the mustard, ¼ cup of olive oil, lemon juice and 1t of salt and pepper. Slice avocadoes lengthwise, covering in the vinaigrette (the lemon juice prevents the avocadoes from oxidizing), then arranging each slice on a platter. Slice grapefruit, adding the segments of fruit in the middle of the avocado. Drizzle rest of vinaigrette, then enjoy!

10. Eggplant Parmesan

This is a delicious take on classic Italian chicken parmesan — feel free to substitute chicken for eggplant. Not only does this eggplant parmesan taste great, it also fills the entire room with aromatic smells while baking. While the cooking time can run over 30 minutes, this is a great dish to enjoy with a bottle of wine. So — open that wine early and enjoy a glass while the kitchen fills with the smell of baked eggplant!
Ingredients:

- 1-2 Eggplants
- 2 cups Breadcrumbs
- 2 cups Parmesan Cheese
- 2 Eggs
- 1tbs Salt / Pepper
- Olive Oil
- 1 jar Marinara Sauce
- 1 box Angel Hair pasta

Directions: slice eggplants lengthwise into 3-4 sections per eggplant, sprinkling the open sides with salt, then dabbing with a paper towel after a few minutes to remove any bitterness. Next, lightly beat eggs, adding ¼ cup of olive oil. Create breadcrumb mixture by adding breadcrumbs, parmesan cheese, minced garlic and salt/pepper into bowl. Dip eggplant into egg mixture, then breadcrumbs. Place on baking tray that is coated in olive oil and bake at 400 degrees for 30-35 minutes. Serve on bed of angel hair pasta, and top with marinara sauce to taste.

Bonus: Grilled Corn on the Cob

My favorite way to eat corn is when it has been grilled to perfection, accompanied by a burger made from South Dakota beef (hopefully not one that had been corn fed!). Thanks to the husk, corn is naturally suited for grilling and requires no additional work.
Ingredients:

• Corn on the cob

Directions: after the grill is up and running, just place the un-husked corn directly on the grate and rotate every minute or so, being careful to not allow any fibers to catch on fire. Seasoned with a little salt and butter, it is tough to beat!

References

Allshouse, J., Kantor, L.S. and Putnam, J. (2002). U.S. Per Capita Food Supply Trends: More Calories, Refined Carbohydrates, and Fats. *FoodReview,* Vol. 25, No. 3, 2-15. USDA Economic Research Service.

Alston, J.M., Summer, D.A. and Vosti, S.A. (2006). Are Agricultural Policies Making Us Fat? Likely Links between Agricultural Policies and Homan Nutrition and Obesity, and Their Policy Implications. *Review of Agricultural Economics*, Vol. 28, No. 3, 313-322.

Beghin, J.C. and Jensen, H.H. (2008). Farm Policies and Added Sugars in US Diets. Iowa State University Center for Agriculture and Rural Development, Working Paper 08-WP 462.

Beydoun, M. and Wang, Y. (2007, July 10). *Obesity Rates Continue to Climb in the United States.* Johns Hopkins Bloomberg School of Public Health, Public Health News Center.

Blisard, N., Stevart, H., and Jolliffe, D. (2004). *Low-Income Household's Expenditures on Fruits and Vegetables.* U.S. Department of Agricultural Economic Research Service. Washington, DC.

Bovard, J. (2006, April 6). *Hoover's Second Wrecking of American Agriculture.* Retrieved March 2, 2008, from http://www.lewrockwell.com/bovard/bovard25.html.

Bovard, J. (1999). Freedom to Farm Washington. The Future of Freedom Foundation. *Freedom Daily.* Accessed 27 March 2009 at http://www.ff.org/freedom/0199d.asp.

Bray, G.A., Nielsen, S.J. and Popkin, B.M. (2004). Consumption of High-Fructose Corn Syrup in Beverages May Play a Role in the Epidemic of Obesity. *American Journal of Clinical Nutrition*, Vol. 79, No. 4, 537-543.

Brownell, K. and Horgen, K.B., (2004). *Food Fight: The Inside Story of the Food Industry, America's Obesity Crisis, and What We Can Do About It.* New York, NY: McGraw-Hill.

Buzby, J. and Farah, H. (2005). *U.S. Food Consumption Up 16 Percent Since 1970.* U.S. Department of Agriculture Economic Research Service.

Chastenet, D. (2005). Economic Factors Affecting the Increase in Obesity in the United States: Differential Response to Price. Masters Dissertation, North Dakota State University, June 2005.

Cohen, S., Gaul, G.M., and Morgan, D. (2006, July 2). Farm Program Pays $1.3 Billion to People Who Don't Farm. *The Washington Post*.

Critser, G. (2004). *Fat Land: How Americans Became the Fattest People in the World*. New York: Mariner Books.

Crumpacker, B. (2006, April 9). You Are What You Eat: A Journalist Traces the Meal on His Plate Back Through the Food Chain [Review of the book *The Omnivore's Dilemma: A Natural History of Four Meals*]. *The Washington Post*.

Drewnowski, A. and Darmon, N. (2005). The Economics of Obesity: Dietary Energy Density and Energy Cost. *American Journal of Clinical Nutrition*, Vol. 82, No. 1. 265S-273S.

Drewnowski, A. and Specter, S.E. (2004). Poverty and Obesity: The Role of Energy Density and Energy Costs. *American Journal of Clinical Nutrition*, Vol. 79, No. 1, 6-16.

Engelgau, M.M., Geiss, L.S., Saaddine, J.B., Boyle, J.P., Benjamin, S.M., Gregg, E.W., et al. (2004). The Evolving Diabetes Burden in the United States. *Annals of Internal Medicine*, Vol. 140, No. 11, 945-951.

Fields, S. (2004). The Fat of the Land: Do Agricultural Subsidies Foster Poor Health? *Environmental Health Perspectives,* Vol. 112, No. 3, A821-A823.

Fite, G. (1960). The McNary-Haugen Episode and the Triple-A. *Journal of Farm Economics*, Vol. 42, No. 5, 1084-1093.

Fogarty, T.A. (2002, January 2). Freedom to Farm? Not Likely. *USA Today*.

Folsom, B. (2006). The Origin of American Farm Subsidies. *The Freeman: Ideas on Liberty*. Accessed 1 April 2008 at http://www.fee.org/pdf/the-freeman/0604Folsom.pdf.

Fraser, J. (2005, July 7). Sugar, High-Fructose Corn Syrup and Type II Diabetes. *Natural News*.

Grunwald, M. (2007, November 2). Why Our Farm Policy is Failing. *Time*.

Hoffman, E. and Libecap, G.D. (1991). Institutional Choice and the Development of U.S. Agricultural Policies in the 1920s. *The Journal of Economic History*, Vol.51, No. 2, 397-411.

Jansen, A.C. (1992). [Review of the book *From New Day to New Deal: American Farm Policy from Hoover to Roosevelt, 1928-1933*]. *American Journal of Agricultural Economics*, Vol. 74, No. 2, 504-506.

Klein, R.W. and Krohm, G. (2007, January 9). A New Season for Crop Subsidies? *The Washington Post*.

Kronstadt, J. (2008). Health and Economic Mobility. The Urban Institute Economic Mobility Report.

Leigh, Suzanne. (2004, December 1). 'Twinkie Tax' Worth a Try in Fight Against Obesity. *USA Today*.

Lincoln, A. (1859). An Address before the Wisconsin State Agricultural Society. Milwaukee, Wisconsin. Accessed March 2, 2008 from http://nal.usda.gov/speccoll/exhibits/lincoln/lincoln_wisconsin.html.

Llewellyn, M. (2004, May 25). Farm Subsidies Contribute to Obesity. *The Stanford Daily*.

MacLean, M. (2002, October 31). When Corn Is King. *The Christian Science Monitor*.

Manning, R. (2004). *Against the Grain: How Agriculture Has Hijacked Civilization*. New York, NY: North Point Press.

Markheim, D. and Riedl, B.M. (2007). *Farm Subsidies, Free Trade, and the Doha Round*. The Heritage Foundation. WebMemo 1337. Washington, DC.

Mokdad, A.H., Ford, E.S., Bowman, B.A., Dietz, W.H., Vinicor, F., Bales, V.S., Marks, J.S., et al. (2003). Prevalence of Obesity, Diabetes, and Obesity-Related Health Risk Factors, 2001. *Journal of the American Medical Association*, Vol. 289, No. 1, 76-79.

National Institute of Diabetes and Digestive Kidney Diseases (2005). *National Diabetes Statistics and Fact Sheet: General Information and National Estimates on Diabetes in the United States*. Bethesda, MD.

Nestle, M. (2002). *Food Politics: How the Food Industry Influences Nutrition and Health*. Berkeley and Los Angeles, CA: University of California Press.

Perez, M. (2008, January 13). *Farm Subsidies are Good Idea, but the System Doesn't Work*. Environmental Working Group. Retrieved on Feb. 25, 2008 from http://www.ewg.org/node/25960.

Philipson, T., Dai, C., Helmchen, L. and Variyan, J.N. (2004). The Economics of Obesity: A Report on the Workshop Held at USDA's Economic Research Bureau. USDA ERS, May 2004.

Philpott, T. (2006, February 22). I'm Hatin' It: How the feds make bad-for-you food cheaper than healthful fare. *Grist Magazine*.

Poirot, C. (2005, December 4). High-fructose Corn Syrup Fueling Obesity Epidemic, Doctors Say. *The Seattle Times*.

Pollan, M. (2003, October 12). The (Agri)Cultural Contradictions of Obesity. *The New York Times*.

———. (2006). *The Omnivore's Dilemma: A Natural History of Four Meals*. New York, NY: Penguin Group.

———. (2007, January 28). Unhappy Meals. *The New York Times*.

———. (2007, April 22). You Are What You Grow. *The New York Times*.

Riedl, B. (2007, June 19). *How Farm Subsidies Harm Taxpayers, Consumers, and Farmers, Too*. The Heritage Foundation. Backgrounder 2042. Washington, DC.

———. (2007, December 13). *Scrap the Senate Farm Bill and Start Over*. The Heritage Foundation. WebMemo 1738. Washington, DC.

———. (2007, July 24). The Dirt on Farm Subsidies. *Los Angeles Times*.

Schlosser, E. (2002). *Fast Food Nation: The Dark Side of the All-American Meal*. New York, NY: Houghton Mifflin.

Schroeter, C., Lusk, J. and Tyner, W. (2005). Determining the Impact of Food Price and Policy Changes on Obesity. Presented at the 97th European Association of Agricultural Economists Seminar, Whiteknights Campus, University of Reading, England, April 21-22.

Severson, K. (2004, February 18). Sugar Coated: We're Drowning in High-Fructose Corn Syrup. Do the Risks Go Beyond Our Waistline? *San Francisco Chronicle*. E1.

Squires, S. (2003, March 11). Sweet but Not So Innocent? *The Washington Post.*

Taubes, G. (2002, July 7). What If It's All Been a Big Fat Lie? *New York Times.*

Tillotson, J.E. (2004). America's Obesity: Conflicting Public Policies, Industrial Economic Development, and Unintended Human Consequences. *Annual Review of Nutrition*, Vol. 24, 617-643.

United States v. Butler, 297 U.S. 1 (1936).

U.S. Department of Agriculture. Economic Research Service. The Economics of Food, Farming, Natural Resources, and Rural America. (2008). Sugar and Sweeteners: Policy. Accessed 27 March 2008 at http://www.ers.usda.gov/Briefing/Sugar/Policy.htm.

U.S. Department of Labor. Bureau of Labor Statistics. Consumer Expenditure Survey. (2006). Accessed 27 March 2008 at http://www.bls.gov/cex/.

U.S. Department of Health and Human Services, National Center for Disease Control and Prevention. (2007). *Physical Activity and Good Nutrition: Essential Elements to Prevent Chronic Diseases and Obesity: At a Glance 2007.* Accessed 1 August 2007 at http://www.cdc.gov/nccdphp/publications/aag/dnpa.htm.

———. (2008). *Diabetes: Disabling Disease to Double by 2050: At a Glance 2008.* Accessed 27 March 2008 at http://www.cdc.gov/.

———. (2007). *Physical Activity and Good Nutrition: Essential Elements to Prevent Chronic Disease and Obesity.* Washington, DC.

U.S. Department of Agricultural and U.S. Department of Health and Human Services. (2005). *Dietary Guidelines for Americans, 2005.* 6th Edition, Washington, DC: U.S. Government Printing Office, January 2005.

U.S. State Department. Protectionism in the Interwar Period. Retrieved March 2, 2008, from http://www.state.gov/r/pa/ho/time/id/17606.htm.

Warner, M. (2006, July 2). A Sweetener With a Bad Rep. *New York Times.*

Williams, A.T. (1997). Estimating the Cost to Consumers of the U.S. Sugar Quota: An Exercise for Introductory Economics Classes. *Journal of Economic Education*, Vol. 28, No. 2, 173-181.

World Bank. (2008, April 14). Food Price Crisis Imperils 100 Million in Poor Countries, Zoellick Says. Accessed 15 April 2008 at http://www.web.worldbank.org.

Young, C.E. and Kantor, L.S. (1999). Moving Toward the Food Guide Pyramid: Implications for U.S. Agriculture. USDA Economic Research Service, Agricultural Economic Report No. 779.

www.ingramcontent.com/pod-product-compliance
Lightning Source LLC
Chambersburg PA
CBHW021823270326
41932CB00007B/311